PARENTS
SEND YOUR CHILD
to College for Free
Successful Strategies that Earn Scholarships

TAMEKA WILLIAMSON

**PARENTS, SEND YOUR CHILD
TO COLLEGE FOR FREE**

Copyright © 2016 by Celestial Enterprises

All rights reserved. No part of this book may be reproduced, stored in retrieval system, or transmitted in any form or by any means without the prior written consent of the Publisher, except in the case of brief quotations embodied in critical articles or reviews.

First Printing under this title: January 2015

Printed in the United States of America

ISBN-13: 978-1-945558-09-2

Celestial Enterprises
BLAZE Leadership Academy
Atlanta, GA
Email: booking@tamekawilliamson.com
www.celestialsent.com

Special discounts are available on bulk quantity purchases by book clubs, associations and special interest groups. For details email: booking@tamekawilliamson.com or call (678) 459-4552

For information logon to:
www.tamekawilliamson.com

PRAISE FOR PARENTS, SEND YOUR CHILD TO COLLEGE FOR FREE

A VALUABLE RESOURCE

"I found this book to be a valuable resource for high school students and their parents as they explore and prepare for post-secondary options."
Shirley C. Kilgore, Ed.D.–Retired Principal/Educational Consultant

IT'S THE PERFECT "GOTO" RESOURCE FOR FAMILIES

"At a time when colleges are capping their enrollments to reduce costs, this guide provides a wonderful comprehensive overview of what it takes for students to strategically prepare for the college admissions process. It's the perfect "go to" resource for families wondering where to start."
Jessica Johnson, Executive Director, Scholarship Academy

AN EXCELLENT GUIDE FOR CHILDREN AND PARENTS

"Tameka Williamson's college prep book is well written. As a former University Coordinator, who worked with At-Risk Children at the University of Missouri, I think this book would be an excellent guide for children, whose parents did not attend college and are not familiar with college life. I think Tameka has done a wonderful job; she has given the potential student an overview or roadmap to college life academically and socially."

Mrs. D. Knight, Stay At Home Mom

A STEP-BY-STEP COLLEGE PREPARATORY GUIDE

"The moment I saw the title for this book, I realized that I had never seen one like this. As teachers, parents, educators, and all who care for, and work with children from all grade levels, we should begin to use terminology that acquaints children with upper level information helping to create upward bound mindsets. We tend to think our children should wait until high school to learn what college preparation is all about. This is a step that should be taken by every grade level. Acquaint our young people about the vocabulary/terminology as soon as they begin to talk. This book does just that. An introduction to College at an early level gives children a mindset that something else is to come after "this." Tameka Williamson has outlined, extraordinarily well, steps for our young ones and their parents to take in preparing for "College Life." I will purchase many of these just to hand out to students and parents. This book will make wonderful gifts to students and parents in lieu of toys and clothes. They will be able to step it up, knowing that "their steps are already ordered.""

Reviewer: **Mrs. Johnson**, Kansas City, Missouri

A MUST READ

"It is clearly evident by this writing that this Author is an advocate of education. Ms. Williamson has a sincere passion to prepare parents, guardians and youth as they seek higher educational opportunities. This book is quite "unique" because it focuses on middle school students as well as high school students. The Author has done her due diligence in researching a number of topics that are instrumental in preparing a young learner for advanced education. After reading this book the reader will have a clear, concise and sound approach in developing a strategy for higher academia endeavors. This book is a must read."

Donna Warfield Fareed, 2005 Amazon Best Selling Author of "Whatever Floats Their Boat"

A WONDERFUL TOOL FOR HIGH SCHOOL STUDENTS AND PARENTS

"Congratulations to Tameka Williamson for the time, effort and expertise devoted to this book. I feel that this book will help students to grasp the realities of college life. This College Preparatory & Planning Guide is a wonderful tool for college bound high school students and parents. I believe that it will benefit a lot of people whether they decide to pursue college or not."

A. McLean, Parent

THE BOOK IS FULL OF SUCH RELEVANT INFORMATION

"The book was purchased for my granddaughter, but I gained some points from it also. It should have been out when started to go to college. The book is full of such relevant information. The book is well written and goes straight to the point."

Dr. Hunt, Parent

BOOK ME TO SPEAK

AT YOUR PTA EVENT, SCHOOL, ORGANIZATION, ETC.

INVITE ME

TO BE YOUR PERSONAL COLLEGE PLANNING COACH

CALL ME NOW

678-459-4552

EMAIL: booking@tamekawilliamson.com

FaceBook: /IamCoachTwill

Twitter: /IamCoachTwill or @IamCoachTwill

LinkedIn: /tamekawilliamson

YouTube: /CoachTwill

JOIN MY EMAIL LIST & RECEIVE FREE RESOURCES

www.tamekawilliamson.com

www.coachtwill.com

ENHANCE YOUR EXPERIENCE AND GET YOUR FREE COPY OF THE COLLEGE FOR FREE ACTION AND RESOURCE GUIDE AT

WWW.COLLEGEFORFREE.INFO

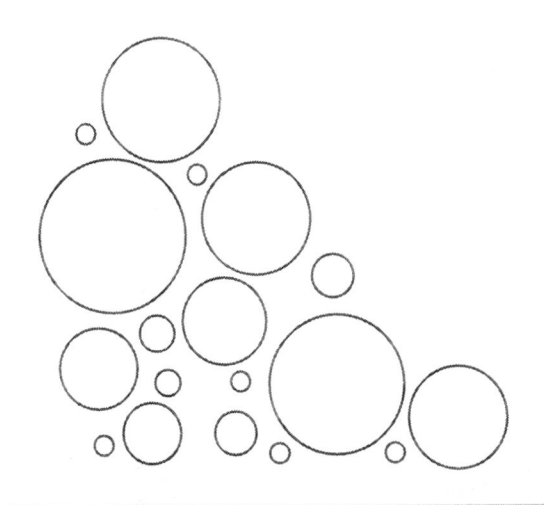

TABLE OF CONTENTS

ACKNOWLEDGEMENTS 11

FOREWORD 13

MESSAGE TO PARENTS 17

INTRODUCTION..23

1. DEVELOPING A COLLEGE AND CAREER
   READY PLAN..29

2. CHOOSING THE RIGHT CAREER 43

3. CHOOSING THE RIGHT SCHOOL 51

4. FINANCIAL AID & PAYING FOR COLLEGE....................83

5. COLLEGE ENTRANCE EXAMS 105

6. MANAGING THEIR SOCIAL MEDIA BRAND................123

7. CONCLUSION 139

APPENDIX..143

GLOSSARY 204

RESOURCES 228

ACKNOWLEDGEMENTS

I would first like to Thank God for orchestrating my life the way He has that's positioned me to live on purpose and make a difference in the lives of families and young people. Now, I have been blessed to help students not only get to college, but secure Free Money for college and succeed in college. Helping students develop as leaders and start building a legacy that gives to the generations to come is a role I am humbled by and don't take lightly. It is for this reason; everything I do and create is dedicated to God, My Mentees, My Families and My Support System.

As always, I am grateful for the continued support of my parents and grandparents. They are always there to encourage me and support me along the way. Thanks to my Fabulous Coach for "sprinkling" his gifts and talents on me and challenging me at every level to become the best me, the one and only Jonathan Sprinkles; My John Maxwell Team Family; My National College Resource Foundation Team; My Accountability Team: Jack. A. Daniels, Jai Stone, Dr. Taunya Lowe, Tracy Washington; Michelle Robinson; My Southern University Family; My Delta Sigma Theta Sorority, Inc. Family; and a host of close family and friends.

FOREWORD

This is My Story.......

God gives us this amazing "gift" in the form of life and we are held accountable for what we do with it. The poem, The Dash, challenges people to reflect on how they will spend their life from the time they are born until the time they die. My goal is to be a good steward of the life entrusted to me and pour out everything I have while on this earth so that I can leave a legacy that keeps giving and allow me to die empty. So, I thank you for investing in yourself and your child by reading my book. It is my hope that you are mentally challenged, intellectually stimulated and spiritually enriched. Get ready to learn about the college admissions process and the successful strategies I use to position my college-bound families to help their kids become both college and career ready. These are the steps necessary for becoming 21st Century Leaders schools are looking for, companies want to employ and who lead successful businesses.

I was a first generation college student, with wonderful parents. My parents had what was classified as a "good" job, with only a high school diploma. But they instilled in me certain values, principles and discipline that molded and shaped me into the person I am today. Although they were supportive of me in all my endeavors, including college, they just didn't know all the tips, rules, practices and steps necessary to bring it to fruition. Nor did they have the funds to cover the expense. This is where the discovery journey began.

Between the library, a college resource center we had in Kansas City for students interested in going to college, friends going through the process with me, teachers and organizations, I was able to at least map out a high level map (Application, Career Selection and Scholarships). Because of my diligence, I was awarded about $2500 in scholarships prior to starting college, with $1500 renewable each year. That number increased when I started doing research as a Timbuktu Scholar to add about $2000 a year. Unfortunately, this was not enough. So the balance was covered by student loans, which I'm still paying for. The other sad reality is that I could have gotten more money if I had started the process earlier (before my senior year) and had higher test scores. You see, I went to a college-prep school and had a 3.7 GPA. When you paired that with my test scores (ACT 19 and 20; SAT, can't remember because I fell asleep during test), I didn't make the cut for an academic scholarship or acceptance into the Honor's College. This could have also prevented the awarding of other funds. The point is, my lack of knowledge at that time is now your guiding light.

My goal is to impart all I know to help families like yours send your child to college without the burden of student loan debt. With the student loan debt crisis in this country and the requirement of some form of college education (trade/technical, 2-year or 4-year) in order for this generation to gain suitable employments, something must be done. Parents, I am serving as their personal college coach and college success strategist so you can learn how to send your child to college for FREE!

By following the practices and strategies in this book, my families have been awarded over Million$ in scholarships and financial aid. I want the same for you.

MESSAGE TO PARENTS

I decided to write this book because I wanted to provide you with a resource to equip you with the tools needed for a successful future. Whether you attend a two-year university, technical college or a four-year institution, 90% of the 21st century jobs will require some form of post-secondary education. Education, now more than ever has become the tool that opens the door that leads to countless opportunities. Unfortunately, the current condition of our educational system has crippled our children, primarily minorities, to be left behind physically, mentally and intellectually. We as parents, a community, family unit, and church must take more of a united front and stand in educating our children. But, the process and ownership must start at home. No longer can we be complacent and dependent on the government and school districts to educate our kids. There must be steps taken at home to enhance the learning experience, hold educational professions accountable and provide supplemental materials that will not only challenge our kids, but inspire them to be the best they can be at every level and have a thirst for knowledge and learning. Our kids are our future and it's our responsibility as parents and leaders to foster that environment for them. That means taking the time to invest in educating them not only on the basics, but expanding their reach by exposing them to global entities (international exchange and learning multiple foreign languages), creating community initiatives, engaging in government and legislature issues, financial literacy and comprehension, creating jobs and opportunities through entrepreneurship, and showing them how math and science can be fun to learn and will open doors for them in the future. In order for their futures to be bright, changes will need to be made in how we prepare them to compete in this global world we live in.

While working in Corporate America I had the opportunity to recruit, interview and mentor young adults. In doing that, I saw the lack of knowledge in their preparation for college, their desire and knowledge of advanced courses, knowing how to conduct themselves in a professional environment and an overall deficiency in their lack of vision and goal setting. Fast forward 5 to 10 years, we now have a generation of students who lack critical thinking, problem solving and professional communication skills. There seemed to be a deterioration in the quality of students graduating from both high school and college available for the workplace – to replace the retiring baby boomers. As a result, Corporate America is afraid and skeptical of the caliber of students being produced to join the workforce. The gap in these professional necessities will require more effort on their part and increase their hiring risk factor.

With the shift in the economy, there was a clear line of those unemployed with a degree and without a degree. The more the global economy move in the direction of a Green Environment, Science, Technology, Engineering, Agriculture/Art, and Mathematics (STE(A)M work environment, the more critical it has become to create a workforce pipeline for these career fields; meaning more educational requirements. Parents don't set your child up to miss the boat on this major shift that has taken place. Without proper preparation and a strong foundation on how to move forward in a direction that will yield opportunities, our children could be left behind.

As your personal "College Coach," this book is an extension of me, designed to provide you as Parents, Group Counselors, Youth and Mentors with a roadmap that outlines what is required for bringing your child's college dreams to life. It will help add clarity to the chaos that exists in the college readiness and college planning process. I don't want students to only settle for getting into college, I want them to succeed in college and become successful leaders in their community. In order for that to happen, there is a need for preparation, as success is predicated on a series of choices and decisions. If one fails to prepare, they are preparing to fail. So, this book will serve as their tool on how to prepare and what steps to take in order to go to the next level of achievement. You will find that the roadmap will outline the required skills necessary to transition successfully from middle school to high school; while providing foundational principles and skills that will aid in succeeding in college and beyond. The key to this all happening is having "a plan." One must plan their work and work their plan as a means of bringing any idea, endeavor or dream to fruition. Let's Get to Work!

It is paramount that we start early in planning for academic achievement, college and real-world readiness. If there is a lack in planning and preparation, there is a high probability students entering college will find it difficult and get discouraged about their future; therefore, dropping out. On the other hand, others will not view college as a viable option. Therefore, the outcome will be them having difficulty securing decent employment and having the foundation and fortitude to create opportunities for themselves. US Department of Labor statistics for 2004 states that those individuals who do not pursue a college degree has a greater chance of encountering obstacles such as unemployment, dependence on social assistance (Vernez, Krop & Rydell, 1999) and incarceration (Harlow, 2001). This has been demonstrated in recent stats on unemployment, incarceration rates and government assistance from 2008-2013.

In an effort to reach the masses, this book is designed to speak to families at all levels, providing practical strategies that will empower parents with the right information to help your child become the driver of their own success, life, and become a unique person of value and significance. My goal is to make what is an overwhelming and complicated process about one of the most important decisions a young person will make in their life, as simple as possible. Being an engineer, certified project manager, and a lean six-sigma black belt, I look at things in terms of processes, order and efficiency. Keeping that in mind, I see college admissions as house. You must first establish a strong foundation that can support the building, before you can add the frame of the house and the roof. As a result, the book is structured that way. First, the focus is on establishing a strong foundation by having students identify who they are: skills, strengths, weaknesses and talents. Once they identify those areas and formulate their goals, they can start building the framework and the roof by exploring the college admissions process from selecting the right career and college, etc. This is where they will begin mapping out the process and developing a plan of action that will position them successfully as college and career ready youth. A house that is built on sand will wash away, but a house built on a solid foundation will withstand the test of time, the winds and the waves. So, we are going to teach your child how to structure their life like a house that can endure all the environmental forces of life. Get their mind ready and let us begin the journey. It all begins with an education beyond high school

INTRODUCTION

He is like a man building a house, which dug down deep and laid the foundation on rock. When a flood came, the torrent struck that house but could not shake it, because it was well built.
Luke 6:48

Everyone use the phrase that our children are our future. But, we must ask ourselves, what kind of future are we setting them up to have? Are we taking an active and proactive role in facilitating their development or are we taking a passive role and sitting on the bench setting them up for failure? The key to any amount of success, whether it's a business, non-profit or personal success, is being grounded and having a strong foundation to build upon. This principle also applies to the development of our children. Their foundation is based on them having a strong educational backing. According to Webster Dictionary, there are several definitions for "foundation," but these are the ones that stuck out the most: 1. the basis or groundwork of anything 2. the natural or prepared ground or base on which some structure rests. I want to bring to their attention the word "prepared." Having a foundation means we have prepared the ground for which everything else stands. With a house, durability comes from building it on a solid rock. The foundation is the support of all other parts of the house and their ability to function properly. In addition, a solid foundation allows the house to be sturdy, in which it can stand the test of time. Just the same, by giving our children a solid educational base, they will have the knowledge and wisdom to function in this world and the ability to address and overcome obstacles they are promised to face.

Sadly enough, the country we live in spends more money on building jails and prisons than on educating our children – the ones who will help our country continue to thrive and exist. Our youth are in a crisis, as well as the educational system and its time to take action. We must own the educational process for our children and not rely solely on the educational system. There is a role families, the community and church play in the process, but we all must work together. This means that we need to look for ways to end the cycle of failure, which is systemic throughout the impoverished inner city communities. Everyone should be involved in the process of ameliorating this situation. If not, this will continue to be the result, but on a higher level:

- "Nearly half of public assistance heads of family are dropouts. Dropouts are three times as likely to receive public assistance as graduates. (more welfare)
- Dropouts are 3.5 times as likely to be arrested as graduates. (more jails)
- Dropouts make up 82 percent of prison inmates. (more prisons)
- Dropouts earn less than one-third as much as graduates." (more welfare)

From Jack Bennett's Opinion News

MESSAGE TO PARENTS

This college success guide will challenge your child to learn more about themselves, how to think and act strategically, while focusing their time on the objectives outlined below in an effort to take them to the next level.

- To increase their understanding of the skills and gifts they possess and how to connect the dots between their skills and gifts to their visions, dreams and career interest
- To increase their understanding of setting goals and developing a pattern of accountability and success practices.
- To increase their understanding of planning and applying the principles to create their own life plan/ business plan and become the driver of their own success.
- To increase their understanding of higher education and the steps required to bringing it into fruition.

After completing the exercises in the book, your child will possess the components necessary to create their personal plan for managing their life, achieving a higher education, turning dreams into reality and accomplishing their goals. Consequently, they will have insight on who they are and the gifts and skills you possess, so, you will understand their purpose in this world and the difference they can make.

As in life, there are many paths one can take in life and each path yields its own outcome. In this process, you will learn that there are many ways in which you can work towards achieving a higher education. There is no single way for managing this process. The key is that a viable plan is crafted for them and managed effectively so they can reap the results. Completing the steps in the following chapters will guide them through the process of determining their personality type, skills and abilities, and see how to align them with potential opportunities in pursuant of their future career and educational endeavors.

At the same time, they will learn to develop new skills and expound on what they have already learned in school, church, home and/or organizations. Too often, youth are gifted with many talents and abilities, but are unable to translate them into real-life and make them work for them in a positive manner. That is why this book starts with identifying gifts, skills and talents as a foundation to build upon. We want sustainable outcomes that have been thought out at the deepest level. The key is to use this book as a catalyst for merging classroom learning with real life experience to forge the best pathway to creating a actualizing a successful future.

NEXT STEPS

Parents, each chapter opens up with learning objectives and an inspiring quote, then it's followed by the chapter content. At the conclusion of the knowledge chapters, you will find an appendix with corresponding activities for students to complete per the material explained in the chapter. The final section is the glossary of common terms you want to familiarize yourself with.

The first thing to do is to go through the chapters and review the information to increase your knowledge. Then have your child read through the material and complete the corresponding worksheets in the Appendix. Hold them accountable and help them use the information as their platform. This is how the plan is developed, which will facilitate your child's ability to implement it.

① DEVELOPING A COLLEGE AND CAREER READY PLAN

"Those who succeed, succeed because they plan. Those who fail, fail because they fail to plan"

Have your child considered what the blueprint of their life should look like? Have they created a vision board that depicts who they want to be, where they want to go, what they want to have and who they want to be with? Well, they will soon have the tools for creating such a plan at the conclusion of this chapter. Their College and Career Ready Plan, or in simpler terms – Life Plan, will serve as their blueprint for achieving their goals, vision and aspirations. It will help them outline their goals, develop a plan of action for achieving them and allow them to see where they will need to make changes, if necessary. The components of a life plan will vary depending on the person. For the stage they are at as a young person, here are some questions that apply to them:

- Where do you want attend school at?
- Where do you want to work?
- Where do you want to live?
- What career path do you want to follow after High School

These questions can appear to be intimidating or hard to think about at one time. Don't fret, the key to creating a plan and setting goals is to take it one step at a time. Once your child accomplishes small goals, they will eventually progress and tackle a larger and more complex goal.

Ultimately, their life plan will focus them and will help them to live a life on purpose and intentionality. By understanding who they are, what they want to do, and why they were created, they can then begin creating a plan that's intentional and committed to answering these questions. They will help them avoid feeling discouraged, disillusioned, wondering where you went wrong, feeling lost and misguided, and/or feeling worthless and wasting time.

WHY IS PLANNING IMPORTANT

Usually, the first step in starting a business is creating a business plan. From there businesses go on to develop strategic plans that focus on how to grow on a yearly basis, which outlines how they will be successful, produce a profit, expand the business, etc. Just like it is important in the business arena, it is equally important in one's personal life. They will apply the same principles.

They may be thinking to themselves, this is some heavy corporate stuff that is way over my head. They may be right. But know that the more knowledge they obtain now about how leaders think and operate, the more likely they will be able to compete globally at all levels. Plus, they are not too young to learn how to be global thinkers and leaders. It's all about college and career readiness. Colleges, universities and scholarship agencies are seeking such leaders. It's all about how they can stand out and add value. To ease their mind, let's look at something more practical. We all like to go on vacation, Right? So, let's go! They are responsible for planning the family vacation 6 months from now. In order for them to have a relaxed and successful vacation, some planning must take place. Planning a successful vacation entails:

Determine a budget
1. Picking a destination
2. Selecting a travel time
3. Deciding on the type of vacation

4. Deciding if the family want a resort, hotel, cruise, or condo
5. Check for travel specials and deals on major travel sites.
6. Research travel retailers and wholesalers — prices, ratings, amenities, etc.
7. Research airline deals
8. Make reservations
9. Identify items needed for trip
10. Pack
11. Leave for their trip

As you can see, everything is a process and steps are required in order to obtain success. Whether you are baking cookies, building a robot, creating a video game or aiming to become valedictorian, it's all centered on a process of steps that are mapped out for execution. Taking it step by step helps you cover all bases, pay attention to detail, and ensure a successful delivery.

WHAT I WANT TO DO WITH MY LIFE

Let's translate this into life, more specifically, getting into the college and career of their choosing. Answer these questions. What are their intentions for their life? How do they plan to spend their time during and after their school matriculation? Do they plan to enter the military, travel, serve in another country with community service or mission organizations, start a business, attend college or all of the above? Whatever the case is, it is important to have an idea(s) of what they want to do in order to develop a successful plan of action that will bring their dreams to life.

Please know that their plans don't have to be an elaborate 5-page booklet, but it does need to be more detailed than, "I plan to travel a year around the world before going to school." They must outline what this year will look like. Where they plan to go, how many places they will visit, what they will do while they are there, how they plan to fund this venture, what they plan to learn and their next steps.

WHAT ARE THEIR GOALS

A goal is a targeted objective intended to be achieved with a defined termination period. Goals provide clarity, direction, motivation and focus.

People who write down specific goals for their future are far more likely to be successful than those who have either unwritten goals or no specific goals at all. The other part of their success is attributed to their ability to not only implement the plan they created, but have the willpower to stick it out when the going gets tough. Achieving goals is not always a smooth path, as there are bound to be obstacles and roadblocks along the way.

Every successful person is a person of goals. Goals **must** be written. Only what is written is what is remembered. Writing down their goals is the first act of commitment to themselves.

> "A man's private philosophy determines his public performance." ***Bishop Dale Bronner***

I've heard my mentor and leaders say, you can tell the level of success a person will obtain when you review their daily agenda. Whatever you deem worthy of doing is worthy to be written down. When determining goals for their life, it is best to break them down into segments. This makes their goals easier to digest. The most common areas people write goals for are:

- Career
- Personal
- Family
- Health
- Spiritual
- Friendship
- Community
- Education
- Financial
- Household
- Relationship

Once they categorize their goals, they must follow the SMARTR model:

S – Specific and have Significance

M – Measurable, motivational, methodical & meaningful

A – Action-oriented and achievable

R – Realistic

T – Time-bound and tangible

R – Relevant to their mission/vision/purpose

For the purpose of focusing on getting to college, they will set goals using the following categories, with the tools and option to include other areas as they go through the journey of life.

- Education

- Career
- Personal

Next, they will segregate their goals in terms of Short-Term (1-90 Days), Mid-Range (3-12 Months), and Long-Range (1-5 Years) goals.

Now, let's explore the goal-setting process by evaluating some questions. They will find a Goal Setting Sheet in the Appendix.

DEVELOPING A COLLEGE AND CAREER READY PLAN

Life plans are as unique as business plans are for organizations and companies. Based on the stage of life they are in, there are varying components they can include. Sample areas of a Life Plan is comprised of:

- Core Values
- Purpose
- Dreams
- Family
- Employees
- Financial
- Friendships
- Fun
- Exit Plan
- Interests
- Location
- Physical Health
- Relationships
- Society/Community Involvement
- Church

- Professional/Career

For the sake of enforcing the learning in this chapter, they will create a life plan in line with what they have learned so far, and the information to come. This will serve as a baseline for them to build upon as they advance in life. As life changes and evolve, so will their plan. It will forever be a living document. For now, their Life Plan will incorporate the following components:

1. Mission
2. Vision
3. Values Statement
4. Goals (Educational, Personal, Career)
5. Short-Term, Mid-Range, and Long-Term Goals
6. Accountability Partners (Mentors, Parents, Coach, etc.)
7. Potential Obstacles
8. Combat Tools

A life plan will help them establish consistency in their life; therefore, intentional and positioned to win. It also creates a system, which has staying power and brings about order. Here are key steps to help them remain consistent in this process:

1. Figure How To Do It
2. Write It Down
3. Practice It
4. Keep Improving It
5. Repeat the process cycle

Life planning sheets for each section can be found in the appendix, allowing them the opportunity to pull the information together into a working document.

MISSION STATEMENT

Writing their personal mission statement results in self-examination and requires them to know who they are. A personal mission statement is a brief description of the direction they want their life to go in, their area of focus, desired accomplishments and aspirations. It enables them to FOCUS their life on a purposed course, eliminating the use of misappropriated energy and time.

F—First Things First, forget about their past

O—Other Things Second

C—Cut the Unimportant (Stop Wasting Time)

U—Unify Behind Their Vision

S—Stick With It

Personal Mission Statements are short-term in nature. They are created to capture their plans at a high level for the next 1 to 3 years.

VISION STATEMENT

Writing a vision means taking a picture, which requires them to focus. A Vision Statement focuses on their futuristic view of what they want their life to look like. Unlike the mission statement, the details of their vision cover the next 5 to 10 years of their life, but they should complement each other.

VALUES STATEMENT

Value Statements are rooted in values and define how they conduct themselves with others, organizations, institutions, or families, etc. Values are traits or qualities they hold in high regard–they serve as the driving forces of their existence. It is part of their moral fabric.

ACCOUNTABILITY PARTNERS

No one person can do anything by themselves. They will need someone to keep them on track, cheer them on, motivate them and even chastise them. So, it is important to think about who is in their life that they can trust to fill these shoes. It must be someone they respect and someone who will be frank, upfront and honest with them. This person can be a parent, a mentor, counselor, coach or even a minister. I also suggest that they select someone currently working in the field they are interested in.

POTENTIAL OBSTACLES

Any person, who plans effectively, anticipates potential pitfalls and obstacles that may occur on their journey. It's the way to being an intentional leader. Granted there will be situations they cannot plan for, but the ability to think forwardly will put them in a better position than someone who hasn't considered the possibility. So, as they process and think through their game-plan, think about the things that can potentially go wrong and derail or delay their plans. Once they identify these challenges, think about ways they can overcome them and continue on their path. They will do this by asking themselves the following questions.

- Is there a viable alternative that can be executed?
- Is there someone I can reach out to who can assist me through this time?

- What am I supposed to learn from this challenge and how will it help me in the long run?
- Is there something I could have done differently to change the outcome?
- How does this goal fit into my master plan?

COMBAT TOOLS

Good soldiers are armed with tools to defend themselves and protect them from harm and danger. The same concept applies to life, business, school, family, etc. One must identify tools that will help them operate on a higher level than everyone else. They must also have the right attitude that is geared at succeeding and doing what it takes regardless of the sacrifice or challenge.

"Problems cannot be solved on the same level they were created." Albert Einstein

Here are some behavioral tools and principles they will need to help them weather the storms of life as they are in pursuit of their aspirations and dreams.

- Set goals and don't be afraid to adjust and adapt
- Eliminate the excuses–they keep them where they are and grant them permission to fail
- Don't wait for something to happen, initiate and take action……Be a Solution – a Change Agent!
- Abstain from complaining – make the best of every situation and find a way to convert the negative to a
- Focus on what they are passionate about
- Know that adversity/challenges are temporary
- Have a support (dream) team

- Have a "Never Give Up" attitude

BECOMING A WELL-ROUNDED STUDENT

This process is beyond just academics. How are you socially, professionally, emotionally and academically presents a total being, not just one unbalanced side? Students setting themselves apart from other students require certain habits, behaviors and even sacrifices. There will be times where they will have to decide whether or not they can go to the mall with their friends or if they are going to volunteer with a youth group because they made a commitment to be there. These types of decisions are part of growing up and being a leader.

An expert on leadership and one of mentors, John Maxwell has published a litany of books with one of them being The 360° Leader. John Maxwell provides recipes for developing and maintaining effective relationships, leaders, attitudes and the equipping of individuals and organizations. For the sake of developing leaders of today, tomorrow and the future, we are going to adapt some of the basic principles he identifies as a necessity in order to stand out as a leader in comparison to an average leader; being a person who is desired by every company and organization. Remember, their goal is to get noticed, admitted, funded and employed. With that in mind, these principles can be parlayed into the educational arena by teaching them the traits they need to be desired by every college and university. Possessing these virtues will endow them, as a student with the edge they will need to thrive in academia, community and professional settings. So, we are going to identify what these principles are and set the stage for excelling in everything life has to offer.

- Adaptability—Quickly Adjusts to Change
- Discernment—Understands the Real Issues
- Perspective—Sees Beyond Their Own Vantage Point
- Communication—Links to All Levels
- Servant hood—Does Whatever It Takes
- Resourcefulness—Finds Creative Ways to Make Things Happen
- Maturity—Put the Team Before Self
- Endurance—Remains Consistent In Character and Competence Over the Long Haul
- Countability—Can Be Counted On When It Counts

Now that they know how to position themselves for greatness, it's time to put the principles into action and create a portfolio that exemplifies each area. Their portfolio will help them stay focused and on purpose, while remaining true to their goals and aspirations. In addition, it can serve as a brag book when they pursue scholarship and/or job opportunities. Here are some examples of things they can do:

- Become an active volunteer and/or member of community organizations, nursing homes, youth centers, etc.
- Create and start a community focused organization that supports a disadvantaged population.
- Go abroad and study in another country for the summer
- Participate in extracurricular activities and take on leadership positions: Student Government, Toastmasters, Science Club, etc.

- Don't settle for mediocre, take advanced, challenging and unique courses: IB/AP Courses, Dual Enroll at a College, Debate, Japanese, Arabic, etc.
- Read and understand business publications such as Wall Street Journal, Forbes, Black Enterprise, etc.
- Start and/or participate in an Investment Club
- Tutor and mentor other students
- Broaden their cultural awareness through music and arts by attending a symphony, opera, art exhibits, museums, etc.
- Participate in thought provoking activities and/or sports such as Chess, Golf, and Cash Flow for Kids, etc.
- Enroll in IB/AP classes in High School and take the required test upon graduation. They can earn college credits upon passing the exam.

This will become the foundation for their life. Now, you and your child should take the time to digest and process the information from this chapter. Take it to heart and begin the planning and development process by completing the corresponding pages in the Appendix.

The goal is to be a well-balanced student with strong demonstration of leadership, academic and community service records. It speaks to who the student is as a person, leader, potential future alumnus and member of the community. It also shows they student cares about others as well as themselves.

2

CHOOSING THE RIGHT CAREER

"The point of life is not to slave away for years until the age of 65 and then say 'Phew, glad that's over!' Rather, it is to make sure that we do not die with our music still in us."

– Lance Secretan

CHOOSING THE RIGHT CAREER

Average Lifetime Earnings:
US Census Bureau

$609,000	No high school diploma
$824,000	High school diploma
$993,000	Some college, no degree
$1,062,000	Associate degree
$1,421,000	Bachelor's degree
$1,619,000	Master's degree
$2,142,000	Doctoral degree
$3,013,000	Professional

Selecting a career choice or vocation is one of the most important decisions they will make in their life. It will set the foundation for how their life progress and the opportunities that will be afforded to them. An important factor in selecting an area of study is to align their decision with something they are passionate about. They never want to make a decision based solely on its monetary value. But base it on their interests, vision, goals, skills and passion. As a result, they will be one step closer towards a purposed driven life—a life that gives them more value, career satisfaction, a sense of accomplishment and a higher level of achievement. They can take a deeper dive by incorporating their values and personality ratings.

To set them on the path of living a life on purpose, we are going to journey through the following stages toward ascertaining a definite career path by focusing only on interest and skills.

Stage 1: Identify Interest and Gifts

Stage 2: Align Interests with Career Fields

Stage 3: Finalizing Career Field

Stage 4: Identify Steps for Pursuing Career Field

Stage 5: Take Action

"Talent alone will not make you a success. Neither will being at the right place at the right time, unless you are ready. The important question is, 'Are you ready?'" Johnny Carson

The Bureau of Labor Statistics reports that men and women hold an average of about 14 jobs by the time they turn 40. Kelly Services, a major temporary staffing agency, reports that almost half of adults are not completely satisfied with the requirements, lack of flexibility, risks and compensation of their current jobs. Many of these individuals will consider changing careers.

STAGE 1: IDENTIFY INTEREST AND GIFTS

The key to career satisfaction is to find an occupation that they can enjoy and excel in at the same time. This can be achieved by matching both their abilities and interests to their desired career field. I would dare them to take it a step further by encouraging them to understand what their purpose is. Understanding why they were created is a fundamental piece of the puzzle of life as it relates to living a full life. For the sake of this section, we are going to focus on their interests and abilities.

1. Who Am I?
2. What Do I Like To Do?
3. What Are My Hobbies?
4. What Am I Good At?

Here are some initial questions they can ask themselves to begin the process. If they never thought about the answers to these questions, that is okay. We are going to explore them and many more on a quest to determine who they are by taking a Career Interest and Career Skills Questionnaire. They will find many personality and skills assessment sites that are free and great at aligning their abilities with potential career fields.

- Interests are defined as those things they are passionate about and feel called to take part in. Examples include ballet, basketball, arcade games, or teaching English to foreign students.
- Skills are things that they are able to do well, such as writing articles, working on car engines, shooting three pointers or giving speeches.

Once they narrow down who they are, what they like to do and the skills they possess, they are ready to move on to the next step and review possible career choices and narrow them down to a final choice.

STAGE 2: ALIGN INTERESTS WITH CAREER FIELDS

Matching their interests and skills/talents with possible careers must happen naturally. Everyone is born with natural gifts and talents that give them the ability to complete special assignments in their life that benefit others.

They will use their results from the questionnaires they completed and narrow down the potential careers that best suit them. Ideally, they will select the top 4 career possibilities where they scored the highest. These will be the top areas that are more in line with what matters most to them and their skill level. From here, they will further review the careers and examine the career options and select the ones that interest them the most. Of all the options, select the 10 occupations they are compelled to learn more about.

Keep in mind there is no perfect process for selecting the "right" career, as there is a chance they can end up with a job that will not incorporate all their interest or use all their skills. At the same time, having this information and completing the process will ensure they are better equipped and educated to making this important decision.

STAGE 3: FINALIZING CAREER FIELD

This stage is about decreasing that potential list from 10 to no more than 3 career choices. They will arrive at this list by investigating the fields and creating a list of things that attract them and those characteristics that are not so attractive. Then they will review the commitments required for each field (On-Call Schedule, Constant Travel, Long Hours, etc.) and decide if they can live up to these requirements.

After asking these questions they should be able to pare down their list and make a final selection. Another point to consider in view of a career field, what is the demand for this field in the next 10 to 20 years? Will there be jobs available? The following resources are available to answer these questions:

- Interviewing family, friends, and others
- Internet
- Occupational Outlook Handbook website
- Library
- Career Centers
- Trade and Business Publications
- Seminars, Trainings, Clubs, Trade Shows or Conferences
- Networking and Mentors

STAGE 4: IDENTIFY STEPS FOR PURSUING CAREER FIELD

Now a decision has been made regarding the preferred career of choice, they will need to know what is required to pursue this profession. Are there certain skills required that they lack such as 4 years of Latin, completion of Physics, Calculus and Computer Programming? Do they need to have 3 years of working as an intern or co-op? Or do they need to have 100 hours of live video production time completed with 10 completed projects. Questions like these will help them map out a plan of execution for bringing their desired career into fruition. They can obtain this information by checking out the resources outlined above, along with speaking to a guidance counselor, mentor, visiting universities or trade schools and by conducting informational interviews with professionals in the field, along with professional organizations.

STAGE 5: TAKE ACTION

They have taken a major step in learning more about who they are and what they have to offer, while discovering how to apply that to a real life decision of selecting a career. It's time to bring the information to reality. Take action and get to moving!

The final component of execution is look for opportunities to volunteer in the career field of choice to get real life experience of working in the field. This will give them valuable insight of what they can expect as far as expectations, potential challenges and minimize the number of misconceptions/unrealistic truths. Finding these opportunities can come by networking with professionals and professional organizations. Remember that an answer to a problem is always a person. So, it is important to engage themselves with a good mentor and network with people aspiring after the same thing and people who are where they want to be. Choose wisely because there are four types of people that exist in this life:

1. People who add to you
2. People who subtract from you
3. People who multiply you
4. People who divide you

It is their choice on the type of people they allow to consume their time, energy and gifts and take up valuable space in what we call their "inner circle." You have to help them make the best decision.

There are some people who live in a dream world, and there are some who face reality; and then there are those who turn one into the other. ~ ***Douglas Everett***

3

CHOOSING THE RIGHT SCHOOL

If you educate a man you educate a person, but if you educate a woman, you educate a family.

― *Rudy Manikan*

Picking a school can be a stressful decision and process, especially with the high student loan debt in this country and questionable job market in some instances. There are many questions running through their head and your minds as parents. You are probably afraid of the unknown: affordability, social lifestyle, safety, quality of education, how to get there, or will you survive? Let me put your mind at ease because this chapter will help you answer all these questions and so much more. So, let's first start with understanding the types of schools that exist.

Because colleges are not a one size fit all model, there are several different types of schools you can attend based on their career interest, class size, financial ability and an ongoing list of classifications. In terms of the type of school, you basically have:

Elite Schools: schools with the most restrictive admission criteria. They consist of about 70 schools and have the following characteristics:

- Highly Competitive–accept fewer than 30% of applicants. You need a high GPA, stellar test scores, superior writing ability and a solid record of extracurricular achievement.
- Often Diverse–they can control the makeup of their student body since they get more applicants than they accept. Students tend to come from all walks of life: upper, middle and lower economic classes, various cultures, races and nationalities.
- Higher Quality of Education–high tuition, large endowments, and many federal grants, the school has the affordability to spend top dollars for top notch

professors, along with having the latest equipment and facilities. Most keep class sizes down and insist on meaningful student-faculty interaction
- Attract Top-Notch People–they draw the best faculty, students, and staff in the business
- Have Large Endowment Funds – stronger ability to offer merit scholarships to qualified students and drastically decrease the large price tag for a quality education

Elite Schools are often referred to as Ivy League schools, but there is also another group of schools in this bunch classified as Public Ivies and "The Other" Elites. Here are some examples of each group.

The Ivy League: consists of the following eight schools

> Brown University
> Columbia University
> Cornell University
> Dartmouth College
> Harvard University
> Princeton University
> University of Pennsylvania
> Yale University

The Public Ivies: public universities that are among the nation's most competitive schools.

> College of William and Mary
> State University of New York at Binghamton
> University of California, Berkeley
> University of California, Los Angeles
> University of Florida

University of Michigan
University of North Carolina
University of Virginia
University of Washington
University of Wisconsin, Madison

Public Ivies are great choices for students who want to attend a highly selective college with state-of-the-art facilities and world class instruction, but can't pony up a small fortune in tuition.

The Other Elites: These are hard to classify elites that are extremely competitive, offer outstanding academic programs, and attract the best and most talented students and faculty.

Bowdoin College
Davidson College in NC
Duke
George Washington University
Juilliard
Macalester College in MN
Massachusetts Institute of Technology (MIT)
Notre Dame
Stanford
United States Military Academy
Vanderbilt
Washington University in MO
Wesleyan University

State Schools: are parts of the university system, are funded largely by tax dollars and they charge considerably less tuition than most private schools. Since they are usually large schools, they have many resources in terms of facilities and personnel. State schools have the following characteristics:

- Big–they can resemble a small city, with thousands of students, teachers, and staff and hundreds of academic disciplines. Everything is oversized from the lecture halls, football games, dances, etc.
- Vary in Selectivity–getting into a top state school outside their home state can be challenging because they limit the number of out-of-state enrollment.
- Serious Resources–they offer just about every class you can imagine, along with access to state-of-the-art facilities.
- Affordable–unless you come from out of state, public universities and colleges offer some of the best deals in higher education.

Within the university system, there is usually a flagship school, which is usually the biggest, most prestigious, and most selective branch of the university. Because they are so large, the flagship universities are often broken down into smaller units, usually known as colleges. Flagship, along with state university systems may also have branch locations across the city and state.

Historically Black Colleges & Universities (HBCU): provide a tight-knit environment that fosters education and a drive for success. These schools can be private, public or liberal arts schools; and are attended mostly by African American students.

Liberal Arts Schools: believe students should work closely with their teachers and should develop critical learning skills and intellectual curiosity. Some liberal arts colleges don't have majors or grades, but they do have requirements.

Liberal Arts Schools have the following characteristics

- Provide Personal Attention–small classes and attentive professors. They emphasize the importance of developing solid speaking and writing skills. You will not find large lecture halls, endless multiple choice exams or teaching assistants.
- Very Selective–there are more than 200 colleges in the US and can be among the most selective schools in the country. They tend to have higher acceptance rates.
- Great Education–they attract the brightest professors and staff in the world. They focus more on teaching and not on publishing compared to large universities. Student's thoughts and opinions are valued.

Most liberal arts colleges are private, but there are some that offer public school prices like Truman State University, Ramapo College and Sonoma State University. The public schools have great reputations that they attract a large number of out-of-state students. Then you have liberal arts colleges that exist within public universities, which give students access to university resources along with the added benefits of smaller class sizes and closer interaction with faculty and other students.

Two-Year Schools: have a diverse student body and small class sizes. This group includes their community and technical colleges, in which some offer four-year degrees. These schools tend to attract students interested in taking classes only, rather than living in a dorm and participating in the social activities. Other students attend as a means to save money, which sometimes serve as a pit stop on their way to a four-year university. Characteristics of two-year schools are:

- Not Necessarily Small–one of the largest colleges in the nation has an enrollment of about 160,000 students (Miami Dade Community College).
- Accepting–they admit majority of their applicants. Typically, you will only need a HS diploma or GED, as they don't usually require an ACT of SAT score. Now they do generally administer assessments to determine class placement.
- Affordable–have significantly less tuition than a public four-year college
- Lack of Personalization–these are usually commuter schools, so they rarely offer dormitories and extensive student services.

Community Colleges are often referred to as Junior Colleges and they primarily offer Associate of Arts (AA) and Associate of Applied Science (AAS) degrees in a wide variety of fields.

Technical Colleges focus primarily on providing specialized skills that will enable students to enter the workforce in lieu of pursuing a four-year degree. Most schools offer a wide range of programs, along with awarding Associate of Technical Arts (ATA) and Associate of Applied Science (AAS) degrees. In finding a technical school, select one with programs that assist with placement into internships or apprenticeships during school matriculation and have a solid reputation for job placement.

Although a degree can be obtained from both types of colleges and can be transferred to a four-year institution, it is recommended to find schools with articulation agreements. This is where the school has contracts with four-year schools that specify which degrees and credits will transfer. You want a program that will allow you to transfer all their credits. Also note, there is a level of difficulty in transferring to highly competitive schools. So, it is important to know their education plan and allowable concessions prior to enrolling.

Specialty Schools: includes trade and proprietary schools that are private, for-profit institutions where students enroll to learn a practical skill required for entry into the workforce. Some of these schools offer both a Bachelor's and Master's degree.

Characteristics of these schools include:

- Focused on Learning–they don't offer many student activities, dormitories or sports. Class sizes are pretty small and can be smaller at liberal arts college
- Pricey–cost more than community and technical colleges and are not likely to offer any federal financial aid.
- Accepting–they rarely turn away students.
- Career Oriented–a good school if you decide to go directly into the workforce, but not so good if you decide to transfer to another school. Credits are difficult to transfer.

Proprietary Schools follow the demands and trends of the workforce, in which they quickly assemble educational programs to match.

Trade Schools focus more on one specific field and offer hands-on training in it. Some popular examples of trade schools include: culinary arts, flight and cosmetology schools. Because of the specific licensure requirements for certain trades according to state regulations, it is critical for you to ensure the school offers the necessary information in their education program.

Distance Learning Schools: with constant advancement in technology as it relates to web interface and communication, more and more schools have embraced this phenomenon and now offer distance learning programs. Response from students has been high so colleges are now offering majority of their programs via TV and the Internet. If you choose to go this route, be sure to research and check their accreditation as a way of avoiding fraudulent programs and illegitimate schools. Characteristics of Distance Learning Schools include:

- Convenient–works well for working adults and people in remote areas of the country
- Accepting–they admit almost everybody who can pay the tuition
- Reputable–a few of the larger schools have regional accreditation to offer legitimate degrees and their students qualify for federal student aid. Some of the more reputable programs have articulation agreements with traditional college campuses so students can transfer credits or degrees.

- Not Always Disembodied–many traditional campuses
- also offer degrees online. This gives you the convenience of distance learning, but also the legitimacy of a traditional school if you are concerned an employer will not take their degree seriously.

THE IMPORTANCE OF ACCREDITATION

I'm sure you have heard the term "accreditation" during their elementary and secondary education term, but probably don't know what it means. Accreditation is basically a set of guidelines and criteria schools go through in order to confer legitimate diplomas and degrees for education completion. The accreditation process is managed and granted by approved agencies, governed by the National Education Association.

This is important for several reasons. First reason is because most of their major corporations check to see if diploma holders come from an actual, accredited university and not a fake or low quality school where almost anybody can get a diploma. Secondly, if you decide to pursue an advanced degree, colleges will turn you down for admission due to a lack of accredited class completion. As a result, you can be forced to repeat classes and spend more money.

You can validate a schools accreditation by requesting to see their credentials in writing and by checking the proper government agencies or the NEA.

FINDING THE BEST SCHOOL

There is plenty of information in books and on the internet to guide you on how to find the best school for their college career. You may not realize this, but this can be a simple process. After you decide on the type of school you would like to attend and determine a field of study, you will then need to assess what is most important to you and select a school that can provide those things. Now don't get me wrong, college rankings according to US News, USA Education Guides and Princeton Review are equally important and serve as a valuable source of information. This information should be used after you complete an internal assessment measuring their personal feelings, needs, beliefs, interests and requirements. So, here are some questions you can ask your child to help determine the best school for them:

1. Do I want to go out of state? If yes, how far do I want to go?
2. Do I want a school that provides personalized teaching settings (small class sizes) or a school with large class room settings?
3. Do I want to attend a one gender school?
4. Is it necessary for me to attend graduate school? Do I want a 5 or 6 year program that gives me a bachelors and masters?
5. What social activities am I interested in (Greek Life, Student Government, Intramural Sports, etc.) participating in?
6. Do I want to go to school in a small town or a metropolitan city?
7. I am a sports fan, do I want a school with a big athletic program?
8. Do I have a strong, average or weak academic profile?

Now that you have challenged your child with some questions to ascertain what they need in order to have a successful college life, you can look at college rankings by various categories to assist you in their final decision. Some of the ranking categories include:

- Best College or University in the USA by Major
- Best College or University in the USA by Location
- Best College or University in the USA by School Type

MAKING THE CUT

There is no limit on the number of schools you can apply for. But keep in mind the fact that each application requires time, energy and money. It is best that you narrow their list down to a manageable number of about 6 schools. You can accomplish this by:

- Talking to friends and family: this will be people you highly respect, preferably graduates of the schools you are interested in.
- Talking to their guidance counselor: they have valuable input to aid you in their decision, along with assisting you with their transcripts, recommendations and other essentials needed for the application.
- Listing their criteria: imagine their ideal school and list what it would look like in terms of academics, location, size, sports, student body, and so on.
- Attending college fairs: identify local fairs at their school, community organizations, local universities, etc. and attend so you can speak to college reps and get brochures/information.

- Requesting school information: go online or call the admissions office to make request and ask for financial aid info also.
- Refine their choices: divide list into 3 categories– dream, target and safe schools
- Stay organized: create a system for tracking the schools you are interested in pursuing

The final action item to aid you in finalizing this decision is the campus visit. Because this can be an expensive task, it is recommended that you conduct visits during their junior and senior years to break up the cost. There are several ways to approach their visits. One way is to target only the schools you are interested in pursuing. Another method is to visit several schools in each category (private, state, specialty, etc.). Then again you can approach their visits geographically by visiting schools by regions, states or cities. It is their decision, but I cannot stress it enough the amount of time and money that goes into campus visits. Yet and still, it is a necessity. Here are some tips to help you with scheduling their visits:

- Check the schools schedule: make sure the college is in session and see if they have special times allocated for visits
- Announce themselves: contact the admissions office and request to sit in on a class or two, interview professors, interview students, setup a meeting with financial aid and the dean of the college of interest.
- Be prepared: be on time for any appointments, have a plan for their visit, and dress neatly, not a suit, but be presentable.

- Explore the campus: someone from the admissions office or a student guide will probably take you on a tour, but be prepared to tour the campus on their own and meet people and get a feel of the environment.
- Stay the night: consider asking to spend the night in a dorm to gain a genuine experience of campus life.
- Go off-campus: visit the surrounding areas of the campus, explore the town or city and identify what is close by like apartments, shopping, bookstores, airport, etc.
- Take notes: write down their observations, thoughts and mental notes about the visit
- Send Thank You notes: after returning home, write and send a thank you notes to all the individuals you met and talked to on the academic staff and faculty. Remain in contact with those you connect it, and continue to expand their network.

HOW DO I GET THERE: THE APPLICATION PROCESS?

Applying for college can be done manually or online. In a world of technology and paper reduction, the preference and most common method is electronic. Besides, completing an electronic application saves time, can save money, gives you immediate confirmation of completion, allows the school to communicate with you and update their application status electronically. You can access a college application by either going to the desired school's website or to one of the college application consortium websites.

- Common Application: www.commonapp.org

- Universal College Application: www.universalcollegeapp.com
- HBCU Common Application: http://commonblackcollegeapp.com/

If you want a paper copy, you would contact the admissions office and request an application packet. Here are some key pointers in completing the application:

- Fill out the application as legibly as possible using a black or blue ink pen if online application is not available
- Allow enough time to complete the application process. Start as early as possible.
- Be aware of all deadlines, requirements, tests needed, recommendations, etc.

In addition, below are some basic Do's and Don'ts when completing the application.

THINGS THEY SHOULD DO

- Read application directions carefully.
- Make sure everything that is supposed to be included is enclosed.
- Fill out their own applications. Type the information themselves to avoid crucial mistakes.
- Start with the simple applications and then progress to the more complex ones.
- Make copies of applications, and practice filling one out before you complete the original.
- Type or neatly print their answers, and then proofread the applications and essays several times for accuracy. Also ask someone else to proofread them for you.

- If asked, describe how you can make a contribution to the schools to which you apply.
- Be truthful, and do not exaggerate their accomplishments.
- Keep a copy of all forms you submit to colleges.
- Be thorough and on time.

THINGS THEY SHOULD NOT DO

- Use correction fluid. If you type their application, use a correctable typewriter or the liftoff strips to correct mistakes. Better yet, fill out their application on line.
- Write in script. If you don't have access to a computer or typewriter, print neatly.
- Leave blank spaces. Missing information may cause their application to be sent back or delayed while admission officers wait for complete information.
- Be unclear. If the question calls for a specific answer, don't try to dodge it by being vague.
- Put it off!
- The application package has two components: the student portion and the high school portion. You would complete the student section and submit it to the respective college/university. The school section will be sent directly from the school and it usually covers the transcript information, a counselor statement, and secondary school report and teacher evaluation forms.

Another part of the student section is the college admission essay and sometimes an entrance interview.

Admissions essay serves as their voice and a way for the selection committee to get to know you beyond the numbers.

Be sure to read the questions carefully and follow directions. It is important for you to brainstorm ideas, create rough drafts, proofread and have several other people read their essay. Highlight their achievements and those characteristics that make you special, unique and deserving of admission.

Interviews are not always required, but serve as another way for the committee to get to know you. Verify with the schools of interest to see if they offer interviews. If they are part of the process, be prepared to articulate who you are in a conversational type environment. Then have a list of questions ready to ask the admissions representative. Also be prepared technologically because some schools conduct interviews using Skype, Google Hangout and other platforms.

The College Admission Essay can be on a variety of topics. Some may ask one specific question, while others may ask you to choose three topics from a longer list of questions. On the other hand, the school may not list any topics and allow you to freestyle with their writing. In any event, the scenario can vary from school to school. You just need to be prepared to cover the basics of writing: grammar, spelling, tense shifts, subject/verb agreement, passive voice, wordiness and punctuation. Because your essay and make or break your admissions process. A strong academic portfolio and a poor essay could impede your acceptance. So, make sure you are mindful of the quality of your essay. Here are seven of the most common types of questions:

1. Choose a significant experience you have had, achievement you have attained, risk you have taken,

or ethical dilemma you have faced, and discuss its impact on you.
2. Discuss some issue of personal, local, national, or international concern and its importance to you.
3. Describe someone who has had a significant influence on you, and explain what that influence has been.
4. Describe a character in fiction, a historical figure, or a creative work (art, music, film, etc.) that has had an important influence on you, and explain that influence.
5. Our campus is enriched by the wide range of our students' academic interests, personal perspectives, and life experiences. Describe a personal experience that illustrates what you would bring to the diversity of a college community, or an encounter that demonstrated the importance of diversity to you.
6. Explain something you have failed in, how it affected you, what you learned and how you bounced back.
7. Explain a difficult situation or a class you were struggling in you had to find a way to overcome. How did you go about overcoming? What did you learn from it?

So, use these questions as a way to brainstorm and stimulate thought about possible topics you can write about. That way, their proactive approach will give you the opportunity to practice what to say, how to say it and how to frame it to be impactful. Ultimately, preparing you to conquer the essay section of the application process and minimizing anxiety and writers block.

Every essay or paper is built using the same structure: Introduction-Body-Conclusion. When dealing with college essays, they can differ from the papers you are accustomed to writing. You will always need a thesis as the central point of their essay. Below are a few sample structures that can be used to write and format the essay.

- Chronological Structure–essays with a chronological structure work forward in time. Their thesis paragraph may start at a dramatic moments, after which the first body paragraph may double back to begin at the beginning.
- Half & Half–describes a cause-and-effect or a before-and-after relationship. The first half will either focus on the cause or on what you were like before an experience, event, or encounter; and the second half will focus on either the effect or on what you were like afterward. The key here is to not focus most of their time describing the experience, event or encounter, but on you and their viewpoints.
- The Three Elements–this is similar to the standard essay structure. Instead of presenting arguments / supporting paragraphs you will describe each point in detail that illustrates who you are.

Last, but not least, here are some essential rules to keep in mind when writing the essay:

- Be a little self-centered. This will be one of the few opportunities they will have to brag and talk about themselves, so take advantage of the situation. The committee wants to know who they are, what they've

accomplished, what impact they made in the lives of others, and where they come from.
- Be specific. Avoid vague phrases and cliché's. Provide clear and concise details and minimize the fluff talk.
- Be aware of the rest of their application. Make sure their essay is consistent with the other parts of their application. Highlight the areas that are not emphasized on their application.
- Be funny and creative, but be careful. Use genuine, but respectful humor. It can add punch to their essay and show that they are smart and human. Showing creativity in their approach can make their essay memorable and impactful.
- Be focused. Do not ramble and appear unfocused. Although creativity is warranted, they must make sure the objective is met and the question is answered. The ultimate goal is to show the admissions officers why they would be a valuable member of their school's academic community.
- Hook them in the first few sentences. It's like reading a good book. If it doesn't catch your attention in the beginning, it will be difficult to continue. In their creativity, find a way to hook them in the beginning and then keep their interest to continue reading.
- Show their personality and be authentic. Admissions officers want to know the student applying to their school. So, convey the message in a relatable fashion that tells them who they really are.

The best way to prepare for the student section and the application process is to prepare a student resume or record of achievement. This is basically their academic portfolio that will be deemed valuable not only during the application process, but also for the scholarship application process. It's what I call their scholarship portfolio, which is a "brag sheet" in plain English. Their resume should include:

- Grade Point Average
- Honor Courses taken
- AP or IB Courses taken
- Standardized Test Scores
- Special Talents
- Academic Awards received
- Sports Accomplishments
- Extracurricular Activities and any positions held
- Organizations or Community initiatives they started, implemented and executed
- Community Service
- Completed College Courses
- College Goals

With social media and technology, there are creative ways to build your college ready resume. You can either search for online portfolio tools or create a LinkedIn account. LinkedIn is a social media platform for professionals who has expanded their audience to include high school students, colleges and universities. Remember, the goal is to be college and career ready. So, LinkedIn would be my suggestion. Besides, it increases visibility to colleges, admissions representatives, companies, etc. It plays into short term and long term goals and vision.

The Admissions Interview is not always required by schools. If they do, it may take place on or off campus with an admissions representative, alum or a student, in person or virtually through the use of technology. Interviews can be stressful and nerve wrecking, but you can overcome this by preparing and practicing. Here are some tips to relieve the stress of the interview process:

- Prepare, but don't memorize–Think about possible questions and how you might respond beforehand. Practice answering as many questions as you can. You will find sample questions in the appendix. Don't commit speeches to memory.
- Dress nicely–You will want to appear professional with a nice business suit or pantsuit in neutral colors (black, nave blue, grey, or brown). A three-piece suit or a prom dress is a bit overboard and flip flops, hoodies, jeans, shorts caps T-shirts, and giant earrings are forbidden.
- Good hygiene–Wash, brush, floss, pluck, shave and deodorize. Go easy on the makeup and cologne/perfume. Do not chew gum.
- Strike the right tone–Be confident, but not cocky or arrogant. You want to be open and genuine, but not inappropriate or rude. No profanity, slang or improper language. Even keep this same presence when you speak to kids on the campus.
- Provide substantial answers–Do not mumble, nor provide closed-ended answers like "yes" or "no" or have a long lapse of silence. Be conversational and thorough answers when responding to the questions.
- Explain–Be prepared to explain any negative or concerning marks on their application, transcripts or

with their test scores without appearing as whining or making excuses. Make sure the explanations are reasonable and sound.
- Ask questions–You will most definitely be asked by the official at the end of the interview if you have any questions for them. "Uh and I don't think so," are not the right answer. See sample questions in the appendix.
- Get educated on the school – What are notable facts about the school? Have they been in the news lately?
- The interview process is not a one-way process, but a two-way process. It is an opportunity for you to learn more about the school and determine if it is a good fit or not, while selling themselves to the admissions officer.

AUDITIONS AND PORTFOLIOS

If you plan to pursue the arts, music or theater fields, in addition to the school band, cheerleading or dance team, you may be required to audition and/or provide a portfolio to the admissions personnel and more than likely to the departmental representative. The following tips and suggestions will help you effectively prepare and show themselves in the best light possible when going through the audition and portfolio process.

MUSIC AUDITIONS

Students who wish to pursue a degree in music–vocal or instrumental, typically must audition. If you're a singer, prepare at least two pieces in contrasting styles. A good way to distinguish themselves is to perform a piece in a foreign language, if possible. Then make their selection from operatic, show music, or art song repertories, and make sure you memorize each piece. If you're an instrumentalist or pianist, be prepared to play scales and arpeggios, at least one etude or technical study, and a solo work. Instrumental audition pieces need not be memorized. In either field, be prepared, ready and able to do sight-reading.

When performing music that is sight-read, you should take time to look over the piece and make certain of the key and time signatures before proceeding with the audition. If you're a singer, you should bring a familiar accompanist to the audition. Seek the advice of their teachers and other students in the department, if possible, to try to acquire audition information up front and early in advance. A great rule of thumb is to know more than is required for the audition and select their audition time and date early.

Practice, Practice, and Practice is critical to the preparation phase. Practice their piece in front of a diverse audience and various times. After each practice performance, seek detailed feedback regarding their delivery, articulation, tone, overall performance, etc. Another way to prepare is to audition and participate in as many performances as possible.

Because programs differ, it is recommended that students contact the college for audition information. In general, music departments seek students who demonstrate technical competence and performance achievement.

Admission to music programs vary in degree of competitiveness, so you should audition at multiple schools, around 3 to 5 schools. This will increase their chance of admittance. The degree of competitiveness varies also by instrument, especially if a renowned musician teaches a certain instrument. Some colleges offer a second audition if you feel you did not audition to their potential. So, be sure to ask if this is offered at their school(s) of choice. Ideally, you would like to be accepted at their first choice, but unfortunately, that may not be the case and you will need to have a contingency plan. Therefore, you will need to make the decision to either pursue a music program at another college or consider another major at that college.

DANCE AUDITIONS

At many four-year colleges, an open class is held the day before auditions. A performance piece that combines improvisation, ballet, modern, and rhythm is taught and then students are expected to perform the piece at auditions. The Dance Assessors look for students to display a level of competence in coordination, technique, rhythm, degree of movement, and body structure. The dance faculty member(s) will also rate their ability to learn and their potential to complete the curriculum. Just like with music auditions, dance programs vary, so the need to check with the college of their choice for specific information is necessary. You should also consider the advice and consultation of area dance professionals familiar with the process.

Band, drill-team, dance team and cheerleading all require auditions and have the same basic principles as outlined for music and dance auditions above. Applicants will be assessed based on their level of competence, technique, coordination, rhythm, etc. The best approach is to have a video portfolio of their performances ready to display and present to the school representatives. Then contact the school to request information concerning requirements, the audition process and auditions dates.

ART PORTFOLIOS

A portfolio is basically a compilation of their presentable artwork. When selecting art pieces to include in their portfolio, you should demonstrate their interest and aptitude for a serious education in the arts. Focusing on these areas and providing the necessary attention in assembling such a package will position you to receive scholarships and compete in national portfolio competitions. Also, be sure their selected pieces show diversity in technique and variety in the subject matter covered. You are given the liberty to showcase any medium – oils, pastels, photography, etc., black and white or color. Please note that their portfolio is not limited to any group of work, but open to any creations you have – classroom, personal drawings, independent projects, etc.

Specialized art colleges typically requests applicants to present about ten pieces of art, but keep in mind the focus is on quality not quantity. Their artwork and transcripts will be reviewed to assess their skill level and aptitude to succeed. Portfolios are typically presented in person; but in the event that doesn't happen, some schools will allow students to mail slides if distance is an issue. With technology, it's easy and almost expected for students to have electronic portfolios, possibly with a following. When dealing with art portfolios, there is no simple formula for success due to the level of creativity, other than a demonstration of hard work. The key is to be able to demonstrate their talent and show a pattern of their skill, commitment to it and passion over time. Lastly, it is important to note that there is no such thing as a "perfect portfolio," nor any specific style or direction to achieve one.

Tips for Pulling Their Portfolio Together:

- Try to make their portfolio as clean and organized as possible.
- It is important to protect their work, but make sure the package you select is easy to handle and does not interfere with the viewing of the artwork
- Drawings that have been rolled up are difficult for the jurors to handle and view. You may shrink-wrap the pieces, but it is not required.
- Avoid loose sheets of paper between pieces
- If you choose to mount or mat their work (not required), use only neutral gray tones, black, or white.
- Never include framed pieces or three smudge
- A slide portfolio should be presented in a standard 8 x 11 plastic slide sleeve, which can be purchased at any photo or camera supply store.
- Be sure paintings are completely dry before you place them in their portfolio.
- Label each piece with their name, address, and high school.
- Theater Auditions

Most liberal arts colleges do not require that students who audition be accepted into the theater department unless the college offers a Bachelor of Fine Arts (B.F.A.) degree in theater. It is important that you apply to the college of their choice prior to scheduling an audition. You should also consider spending a full day on campus so that you may talk with theater faculty members and students, attend classes, meet with their admission counselor, and tour the facilities. If possible, do this prior to their audition as a means of building rapport and getting a better feel of the environment.

Although each college and university has different requirements, you should prepare two contrasting monologues taken from plays of their choice if you're auditioning for a B.F.A. acting program. Musical theater requirements generally consist of one up-temp musical selection and one ballad as well as one monologue from a play or musical of their choice. The total of all their pieces should not exceed 5 minutes. Music for the accompanist, a resume of their theater experience, and a photo are also required.

Tips to Get You Successfully through an Audition:

- Choose material suitable for their age.
- If you choose their monologue from a book of monologues, you should read the entire play and be familiar with the context of their selection.
- Select a monologue that allows you to speak directly to another person; you should play only one character.
- Memorize you selection.
- Avoid using characterization or style, as they tend to trap you rather than tapping deeper into inner resources.
- As a last note, schools are starting to implement required reading lists. So, contact their school of choice to identify if this is a requirement and what the list entails.

Afterwards, the only thing left to do is to apply for college and get that acceptance letter in the mail or email.

ENHANCE YOUR EXPERIENCE AND GET YOUR FREE COPY OF THE COLLEGE FOR FREE ACTION AND RESOURCE GUIDE AT

WWW.COLLEGEFORFREE.INFO

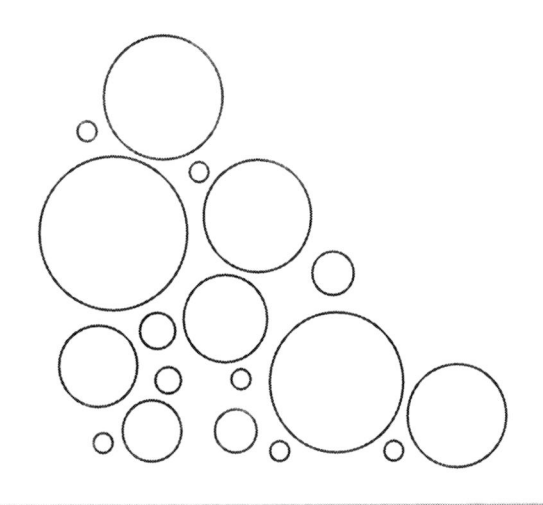

4

FINANCIAL AID & PAYING FOR COLLEGE

Tell me and I'll forget. Show me, and I may not remember. Involve me, and I'll understand.

– Native American saying

Financial Aid basically fills in the gap from the cost of college and what you as a family is expected to pay. You will complete an application providing information on your assets and availability of money. The government with then determine how much money your family is eligible for and will receive toward your child's college education. Based on your application, they will either offer you "free" money in the form of scholarships and grants, or they will offer you loans—which have to be paid back. This will either cover all of their expenses or a portion of it and you will be responsible for the rest.

Before we dig deeper into the types of financial aid and other forms of funding for their education, let us take a look at some basic terminology you will encounter throughout this process.

TERMS AND LANGUAGE

The financial aid process can be confusing to some, especially when it comes to the language used in the applications and informational packets. Because the process of applying for financial aid is a competition, with thousands of students vying for the same pot of money, it is important to have a clear understanding of what you are getting themselves into. Here are common terms and acronyms you and their family need to know and understand.

Basic Acronyms:

> COA: Cost of Attendance
> EFC: Expected Family Contribution
> FAA: Financial Aid Administrator

FAFSA: Free Application for Federal Student Aid
FWS: Federal Work Study Program
PLUS: Parent Loan for Undergraduate Students
SAP: Satisfactory Academic Progress
SAR: Student Aid Report
SEOG: Supplemental Educational Opportunity Grant

NEED

The main purpose of the FAFSA is to determine their level of need. This is defined by the Department of Education as the difference between how much college costs (COA) and how much you can actually pay (EFC). So, the formula is: Need = COA–EFC

COST OF ATTENDANCE (COA)

COA is the total cost required for you to attend their college of choice per year. As described in the previous modules, tuition costs vary based on the type of school. Therefore, the COA will be affected also. At most private schools, tuition is the dominate factor in COA; whereas, room and board is the overarching number for many public schools.

When estimating COA, you will look at the following areas:

- Tuition
- Room and Board
- Fees
- Books
- Living Expenses
- Meals
- Transportation
- Personal Expenses

- Dependent Care
- Computer Purchase
- Costs related to a Disability or Medical Condition
- Costs for Eligible Study Abroad Program
- Entertainment

As COA relates to financial aid and determining need, the higher the estimate, the better. A high COA will give the assumption that their need is greater, which makes you eligible for more need-based aid.

EXPECTED FAMILY CONTRIBUTION (EFC)

As stated, EFC is determined by the Department of Education and it is their perception of what they "think" you can pay towards a college education. Depending on how much you and their family have in assets, savings, investments, and how accurately you complete the FAFSA, their EFC can be any number under 999,999. The number may feel like it is high, don't worry because there is non-need based aid available.

You may still be wondering how EFC is determined. When you fill out the FAFSA, it requires you to provide personal information such as family size, marital status, and number of dependents, income and assets. An organization known as the Federal Processor calculates their level of eligibility for financial aid using the "federal methodology."

Please note that many schools, typically Ivy's, require additional information with the FAFSA to determine need and eligibility for non-federal aid, such as completion of a Financial Aid CSS Profile. Plus colleges usually have their own financial aid forms and base their decision on what they call the "institutional methodology." This is often a stricter process that takes into account the value of any property in addition to their assets, which the FAFSA does not do. So, it is important to find out the requirements for the school you are seeking application for. That is why it is important to contact the school immediately once you have decided upon a college/university. In addition, find out their required deadlines to allow ample time for completion, as it may differ from the federal deadline. The earlier you submit your child's applications, the better. Please note, all schools are not equal when it comes to financial aid because they have different guidelines, distribute monies differently and fund students differently.

NEED-BASED AID

Now that you know Need = COA–EFC, you should also know that grades, activities, and test scores has no bearings on need-based aid.

If it is determined that you have a need because their EFC is lower than the COA, you will qualify for the following need-based aid:

- Pell Grants–Largest source of need-based aid. Awarded to those with greatest need)
- Supplemental Educational Opportunity Grants (SEOG)–those with the most financial need, usually Pell Grant recipients
- Perkins Loans
- Academic Competitiveness Awards–visit www.ed.gov and search for ACG State Programs

- National SMART (Science and Mathematics Access to Retain Talent) Grants
- Most College Work Study
- Most State Grants–visit www.ed.gov/erod and click on their state/territory
- The Subsidized Portion of the Stafford Loan
- Scholarships and Tuition Waivers

NON-NEED BASED AID

This is aid that includes awards, scholarships, and tuition waivers based on merit or other factors, including academics, athletics and musical talents. Federal sources for non-need based aid include Unsubsidized Stafford Loans and the Parent Loans for Undergraduate Students (PLUS). Although these are helpful resources, they are the least desirable because they have stricter repayment policies than the Perkins Loan and Subsidized Stafford Loans.

You may be wondering what the difference between these loan options is.

The PLUS Loan – a parent loan backed by federal government and carries a higher interest rate than the other loans. Repayment begins 30 to 45 days after the loan is made.

- Unsubsidized Stafford Loan–guaranteed by federal government and starts accruing interest while the child is still in school
- The Subsidized Stafford Loan–guaranteed by federal government and doesn't start accruing interest until six-months after the child graduates.

- Perkins Loan–low-interest loan guaranteed by the government and granted to students with the most financial need

Be sure to investigate all options prior to signing any paperwork and choose wisely.

FINANCIAL AID FORMS

The greatest challenge of the financial aid process is understanding and mastering the completion of the FAFSA. Although, the form may appear intimidating and requires too much personal information, don't let it keep you from applying for aid. Believe or not, the form has gotten easier over the years as technology has evolved. The following information is provided to help you understand the basics. Plus, there are many resources available to assist you with the process. You have the Department of Education student website, www.studentaid.ed.gov, the Federal Student Aid Information Center, 1-800-4-FED-AID (1-800-433-3243), and you can reach out to their guidance counselor or financial aid counselors at the school. Do not pay anyone for assistance with completing the form. You can seek the assistance of qualified financial advisors and/or college planners to help you strategize, re-align their assets and legally worth through the loop holes that decrease their EFC and drastically increase their reward.

STUDENT AID REPORT (SAR)

This is the report you will receive back from the Department of Education after completing and submitting the FAFSA. The SAR will provide you with their EFC. So, you will want to apply as early as possible in order to receive their EFC in enough time to plan accordingly. Their EFC tells you whether you are eligible for certain kinds of financial aid, along with informing you of their overall level of need. It is highly recommended that you complete and submit their FAFSA electronically because it is free, efficient and faster than the paper and snail mail process.

THE PROFILE

As stated before, many schools require an additional form known as the College Scholarship Services (CSS)/Financial Aid PROFILE Application. Schools require this supplemental application because they believe the FAFSA is too simple and don't request enough information. The PROFILE takes into account additional assets not provided on the FAFSA such as their parents' home equity amount in their primary residence. Consequently, students qualify for less aid. Now there will be an opportunity to explain why you qualify for more financial aid, but know that there is a fee to complete the PROFILE.

DEADLINES

Time is of the essence when applying for financial aid. In the beginning, it was stated that the process is a competition. Most of the time when students miss out on financial aid, it is because they waited till the last minute to file or failed to submit any corrections in a timely manner.

Each school will have its own deadline for both federal and institutional aid, along with deadlines for scholarships. It is in your best interest to apply at the earliest date possible, even if you have to estimate their financial figures. The FAFSA used to be available January 1st of each year. With the recent change, it is now available earlier to offer more benefits to families and schools. October 1st is the new availability date for families to submit their FAFSA application. For this new process, families will report income and tax information from an earlier tax year. See the following table for a summary of key dates provided by the Department of Education FAFSA website.

When a Student Is Attending College (School Year)	When a Student Can Submit a FAFSA	Which Year's Income and Tax Information Is Required
July 1, 2015–June 30, 2016	January 1, 2015–June 30, 2016	2014
July 1, 2016–June 30, 2017	January 1, 2016–June 30, 2017	2015
July 1, 2017–June 30, 2018	October 1, 2016–June 30, 2018	2015
July 1, 2018–June 30, 2019	October 1, 2017–June 30, 2019	2016

Again, I can't stress it enough. It is recommended that you apply early. It's like the old adage; the early bird gets the worm. The sooner you file, the better your chances are of being considered for limited funds.

OTHER FUNDING RESOURCES

Planning ahead can make all the difference when it comes to paying for college. The more time you allow themselves to plan, save and invest, the more you can accumulate. This constitutes developing a long-term financial plan utilizing the various savings plan and investment options.

First and foremost, the most important task your child can achieve to aid in paying for college is to perform well in high school and work hard to achieve high scholastic achievement, along with garnering high test scores on their PSAT, SAT and/or ACT. Another contributing factor is their involvement in extracurricular activities. It is important to have a diversified portfolio of activities where you actively participate, and hold offices, along with volunteering with community organizations. All of these activities help you create a strong scholarship portfolio that can open the door to multiple scholarship opportunities and leads. Don't wait until their junior and senior year to focus on participating in these areas. Starting early allows you to start searching and identifying possible scholarships prior to applying for them. Every hour of community service and every tenth of a grade point you earn as a freshman, sophomore, and junior in high school can lead you to potential scholarships.

529 PLANS

Allow you the opportunity to pay now for their future tuition. The earlier you start saving money through this plan, the better off you will be. Section 529 Plan is an IRS Code that serves as a tax advantaged investment plan designed to encourage families to save for college. 529 Plan did for higher education what the 401K did for retirement. You can find explicit details in your state by visiting the College Savings Plans Network (CSPN) website at www.collegesavings.org or by calling 1-877-277-6496.

There are 2 types of 529 Plans: Prepaid Tuition Plans and Savings Plans.

1. Pre-paid Tuition Plans allows you to pre-purchase a defined amount of tuition today—either in years or credits based on today's rates for attendance at an institution of higher education tomorrow. This allows you to attend college later without having to pay the increased cost of tuition. Details of this plan vary from state to state. Only offered in 13 states.
2. Savings Plans allow families to save in a variety of investment vehicles with many options, including equity-based investment options, stable value, guaranteed options, and/or certificate of deposit based options. Most 529 plans offer a variety of age-based investment options where the underlying investments become more conservative as the beneficiary gets closer to college age. Currently offered in all 50 states.

As with anything, there are pros and cons to what is being offered. In this case, here are some of the benefits and caveats.

529 PROS

- Earnings grow tax-deferred
- Distributions are tax-exempt when used for college costs
- Accounts benefit from state-tax exemptions or deductions
- Can be opened for both relatives and friends
- Can choose how their money is invested in the savings plan
- Accounts can be transferred to other family members

- Accounts and be refunded, but with penalties
- There are no income limitations governing who can
- open a 529 plan
- IRS gift-tax rules offer an accelerated giving benefit
- You have fewer limits for use than you do with other college savings plans

529 CONS

- Plan fees may make this a poor choice for short-term planning
- Withdrawing funds results in a 10% penalty
- Funds used for anything outside of school will be taxed
- Prepaid tuition plans may reduce eligibility for other financial aid
- College savings plan accounts in their name will be assessed at 20%
- Prepaid tuition plan funds must be used within a limited time period
- Time extension may come with a penalty
- Funds can't be used for most foreign schools
- Funds can't be used for schools not considered "eligible" institutions of higher education

COVERDELL ESAS

The Coverdell Education Savings Account, formerly known as the Education IRA, is another viable option for long-term college savings planning. These accounts are extremely flexible and offer marked advantages over the 529 plans. Just as the 529, there are drawbacks and benefits.

COVERDELL PROS
- Unlimited investment options
- Few limits are placed on where the funds may be used
- These accounts may be set up at any brokerage firm
- No expiration date for Coverdell tax benefits
- Withdrawals for qualified educational expenses are tax-free

COVERDELL CONS
- $2,000 annual contribution limit.
- Charged varying setup fees and other administrative costs
- There are income limitations on who may participate
- Accounts are counted as a student asset in the needs-analysis formula, which greatly reduces other aid eligibility.
- Funds generally must be used before the student reaches 30 years of age.

OTHER PLANS

Outside of the 529 and Coverdell ESA plans, you can utilize their own investments and/or map out viable options with their financial planner. In addition, you have the following two options to include in their long-term planning strategy.

- Custodial Accounts–also known as Uniform Gift to Minors Act (UGMA) accounts or Uniform Transfer to Minors Act (UTMA) accounts. These plans can be set up with any brokerage firm or mutual fund company. There are tax advantages for this plan, along with a benefit rate at which the account earnings are taxed. The first $750 is exempt, the next $750 is taxed at the child's lower federal rate, and anything beyond is taxed at the custodian's federal rate. To qualify, you must be younger than 14. Once you reach an age between 18 to 25, contingent upon the state requirements, all funds in the account become their property and you are legally entitled to spend the money on anything you want—not just college. Savings Bonds are backed by the full faith and credit of the US government. They offer as many of the same benefits, including tax exemption when used to cover the costs of education.

- Now, if you find yourself not in a position to start early and you are late in the game, there are potential options for you to review and pursue.

Tax Strategies–looks at how you fill out your tax forms. By focusing on minimizing the income and assets you report during the year before they start college is important and beneficial.

- Education Tax Credits–you and their parents may qualify for one of the Taxpayer Relief Act of 1997 programs
  - $1500 Hope Credit is where parents get a 100% tax credit for the initial $1100 of their tuition and a 50% credit for the next $1100. This credit is phased out for joint filers earning between $90K—$110K, or for single filers earning between $45K—$55K.
  - $2000 Lifetime Learning Credit represents a 20% tax credit for the first $10K of their tuition. There is no two-year limit, and parents can claim this credit

even when your child goes to graduate school. The same income levels apply as the Hope Scholarship.

You can visit www.irs.gov and download form 8863 for details and any recent changes.

- Student Income Protection is to minimize the number of assets listed in their name. Student income is assessed with stricter rules because of the lack of need for you to use their earnings to pay for household needs, such as food and shelter. Therefore, parents should never put assets in their name. Student income is protected up to $3000. Anything a dependent earns above this amount is assessed at 50% when it comes to financial aid eligibility. Basically, you are better off not working the year before you enter college if you will earn more than $3000. Exceptions to this rule are either jobs or spending opportunities that are considered exempt such as:
- Get a work–study job
  - Spend their allowance or on-hand cash immediately on college necessities
  - Pay down any consumer debt
  - Join AmeriCorps because their earnings are exempt from EFC because you can earn up to $9450 in college assistance for two years of AmeriCorps service.

Please note the terms of these plans and strategies can change as legislature and laws change. So, always get the latest information by reviewing the Department of Education website, their state website and/or consult a tax accountant or financial advisor for accurate details.

DECLARING DEPENDENCY

Your child may say they are providing for themselves and funding their lifestyle and way to college. Therefore, you feel your income status is not applicable to their financial aid application, which means thwy can get more money. The Department of Education will not declare your child as "independent" and no longer include your income and assets when calculating financial aid unless you can answer "yes" to any of the following questions:

1. Will you be 24 years old by January 1 of the current school year?
2. At the beginning of the current school year, will you be working on a master's or doctorate degree?
3. As of today, are you married?
4. Do you have children who receive more than half of their support from you?
5. Do you have dependents that live with you and receive more
6. than half of their support from you, and will do so until the end of the school year?
7. Are both of their parents deceased? Are you, or were you until the age of 18, an orphan or a ward of the court?
8. Are you currently serving on an active duty in the US Armed Forces for purposes other than training?
9. Are you a veteran of the US Armed Forces?

As you see there are fewer options when you compare long-term planning with short-term planning strategies. The key is to be prepared and strategic in their approach when it comes to funding.

WHERE IS THE FREE MONEY?

Positioning your child to receive what is classified as FREE money in the forms of grants and scholarships requires preparation and knowledge of what is out there and where to find it. Their ultimate goal and desire is to get someone else to fund their college education. That means you not only want to rely on aid from the school and government, you will want to search for scholarships provided by corporations, private and public organizations. FREE money can come in many forms such as: Federal grants, State grants, Private scholarships, and Institutional scholarships, Federal scholarships, Service awards, Fellowships, Tuition waivers, Housing allowances and Forgivable loans. So, you must be ready to identify the right people, organizations and groups and start networking.

SCHOLARSHIPS

Scholarships can be won for any number of accomplishments, including academics, athletics or even music. Scholarships are either categorized as a general funding source or they have specific qualification categories such as ethnicity, degree majors, gender, organization affiliation, disability, etc. They come in the form of private, institutional and federal.

Private scholarships can come from anyone and anywhere for any number of reasons. You generally have to pursue these scholarships on their own, independent of the college you apply to. Keep in mind most colleges count private scholarships as aid when calculating their financial aid award. For this reason it is good to compare multiple colleges to determine how they classify private scholarships when determining their overall level of need for financial aid—will it decrease the amount of financial aid you are eligible for or will it be excluded from the overall formula.

Institutional scholarships typically come from the college's endowment or foundation, in which the financial aid offices will definitely count it as aid in their total financial aid need determination. Just like private scholarships, you should ask the financial aid officer how the award will affect other financial aid you qualify for and receive.

Federal scholarships are federally funded scholarship programs. Some examples of these types of scholarships are The Byrd Scholarship (www.ed.gov/programs/iduesbyrd) and the Truman Scholarship (www.truman.gov). Because most of these scholarships are not highly publicized, it is recommended that you become familiar with the Department of Education website (www.ed.gov) and search for "scholarships" on the internet. In addition, you can find valuable scholarship information and application information on the following free scholarship search engines:

1. www.fastweb.com
2. www.studentaid.ed.gov
3. www.scholarshipamerica.org
4. www.collegenet.com
5. www.wiredscholar.com
6. www.gocollege.com
7. www.fastaid.com
8. www.collegeview.com
9. www.collegboard.com
10. www.scholarships.com

Scholarship Contests offers you a chance to roll the dice and compete for a chance to win scholarship dollars. Before applying, be warned and skeptical of any contest that has any fees involved. Here is a sample list of legitimate and free, scholarship contests:

1. National Peace Essay Contest (www.usip.org)
2. Holocaust Remembrance Project (www.holocaust.hklaw.com)
3. The Better Earth Environmental Essay Contest (www.abetterearth.org)
4. Society for Professional Journalists (www.spj.org/a-hs.asp)
5. Coca-Cola Scholars Foundation contest (www.coca-colascholars.org)
6. Abraham Lincoln Contest (www.thelincolnforum.org)
7. John F. Kennedy (www.jfkcontest.org)
8. Ayn Rand (www.aynrand.org)
9. Duck Tape Club (www.ducktapeclub.com)
10. The National Endowment for the Humanities (www.wethepeople.gov)

Memorial Assistance is memorial scholarships offered to assist those affected by national tragedies or relatives of police officers, firefighter or soldiers who lost their lives in the line of duty. You should search their state higher education boards for assistance if you fall under one or more of these categories.

As a note of caution, be aware of scholarship scams. Most scams ask for payments up front and guarantee you will receive money for college, which is not true. Any legitimate source will never require you to pay a fee and there are no guarantees when it comes to scholarship awards.

SERVICE AWARDS

Service Awards are given to individuals who dedicate their time, life and efforts to others. Not only is there a financial reward in doing so, it looks good on their resume when it comes to applying for jobs. Let's take a look at the types of service awards you can go after.

AmeriCorps offers up to $10k in scholarships for those who perform community service. If AmeriCorps money is used to repay student loans, you do not have to report it to the financial aid office. Therefore, it will not decrease their financial aid dollars. Visit www.americorps.org for details

Armed Forces can be very rewarding when it comes to paying for their college education. They publicize that you can earn as much as $50,000 for college depending on the branch of service you choose, but other factors include length of service in the military, how long you attend college and what kind of degree you pursue. Although the dollars are enticing, be sure to read, dissect and understand what is expected of you and the level of commitment you must make. Then make sure you can live up to the requirements prior to signing on the dotted line. If you do decide this is the path to take, contact their school of choice to find out if they have a financial aid officer who specializes in veteran's administration (VA) benefits, as VA benefits on their financial aid can be very complicated.

Another option is the Reserve Officers Training Corps (ROTC), which provides tuition expenses and a $100 monthly stipend. ROTC requires that participants serve in the armed forces after graduation.

Then you have the service academies that provide free tuition, but they are highly selective and require five years of service in the military. At the same time, if you are serious about the military and really interested in getting a free education, there is no better choice.

Here are the four service academies for you to explore if interested:

- The U.S. Military Academy (West Point, New York)
- The U.S. Naval Academy (Annapolis, Maryland)
- The U.S. Air Force Academy (Colorado Springs, Colorado)
- The U.S. Coast Guard Academy (New London, Connecticut)

Fellowships are free money that comes in the form of a stipend awarded for a specific purpose, skill, need, or project. Fellowships are generally associated with graduate studies, but there many available for undergraduates. This type of aid will not be found in their typical scholarship books and websites because they are funded by community-based and nonprofit groups who merge their philanthropic giving with educational opportunities. So, you will have to be savvier with their search in finding these dollars.

MAKING THE BEST DECISION

Money is usually the driving factor in most decisions, especially when it comes to a high-ticket investment like a college education. You want to make sure that the school offering you the aid also provides the total academic package you need. It is not advantageous for you to select a school because they gave you the most money, but they lack the academic program/classes you desire to pursue or the school can have the prestige you want, but they are offering you a small financial aid package–leaving you with an enormous amount of post-college debt. The choice is theirs, choose wisely. Just make sure you weigh all their options and make an informed decision that will support their life plan and goals. Seek the advice of a highly respected mentor, counselor or friend if need be.

Once the decision is made, you will need to sign and submit their acceptance letter. You can accept the total offer or you can decide to only accept part of the package. For example, the school may offer both grants, scholarships and loans and you may decide to only take the grants and scholarships. Whatever you decide, make sure you have the full picture on their total COA to determine whether or not you have enough money to cover those expenses. If you do choose to accept a loan, borrow wisely by only taking out what you need. Do not look at this as an opportunity to spend frivolously on unnecessary items such as: clothes, cars, trips, gadgets, etc. In the event you decline the option to take out a loan, know that you can always reapply if you later find out it is needed to cover their expenses.

5

COLLEGE ENTRANCE EXAMS

Today's preparation determines tomorrow's achievement.

- Unknown Source

Hearing the word "test" may send your child and even you into a nervous tail-spin. Unfortunately, it is a reality of life and one of the main components for getting accepted into a major college/university. The SAT and ACT are the main two tests used to determine college admissions and scholarship rewards. Prior to taking either one of these tests, you will take the PSAT–a preliminary version of the SAT. All three tests is a measurement of their achievement in Math, Reading, Writing, English and Science. Let's take a look at each test individually. Before we do that, note that the best way to maximize the benefits of taking these test is to prepare for it. Even if your child is an honor student, they still need to study and understand the intricacies of the test and their test strategies. So how should your child prepare? The best way is for them to:

- Take challenging courses at school
- Do their homework
- Prepare for tests and quizzes
- Ask and answer practice questions
- Get a tutor
- Take a test prep class

Now, we can look at the types of test your child would need to prepare for.

- PSAT/ NMSQT (www.collegeboard.com/student/testing/psat/about.html)
- The Preliminary SAT/National Merit Scholarship Qualifying Test is a program co-sponsored by the College Board and National Merit Scholarship Corporation (NMSC). It is a standardized test that provides firsthand practice for the SAT, along with the

opportunity to enter NMSC (www.nationalmerit.org) scholarship programs and gain access to college and career planning tools.

The PSAT/NMSQT measures: critical reading, math problem-solving, and writing skills. It is a measurement of the skills acquired over the years both in and out of school, not specific facts from their classes.

There are several benefits to taking the PSAT/NMSQT:

- Receive feedback on their strengths and weaknesses on skills necessary for college study
- See how their performance on an admissions test might compare with that of others apply to college
- Enter the competition for scholarships from NMSC during their Junior Year of High School
- Help prepare you for the SAT
- Receive information from colleges when you check "yes" to Student Search Service

It is recommended that your child take the PSAT/NMSQT during their sophomore year to give them a preliminary feel of what is on the test and an idea of the areas they need to focus on prior to taking it during their Junior Year, when it really matters because it determines whether or not they qualify for the National Merit Scholarship.

There is also the PSAT 10. PSAT/NMSQT and PSAT 10 are basically the same test, offered at different times of the year. Here are the common benefits outlined by CollegeBoard:

- They are both great practice for the SAT because they test the same skills and knowledge as the SAT — in a way that makes sense for your grade level.

- They both provide score reports you can use to personalize your Khan Academy® SAT practice.
- These score reports also list which AP courses you should check out.

You should speak to your child's counselor on identifying the best test to take. Or you can have them take it in 10th grade as a dry run and preparation run for the 11th grade. Here are some notable differences outlined by CollegeBoard:

PSAT/NMSQT vs. PSAT 10		
Facts and Features	PSAT/NMSQT	PSAT 10
Who takes the test?	10th- and 11th-graders	10th-graders
Where do students take it?	At school	At school
When do students take it?	Wed., Oct. 19, 2016. Other options: Sat, Oct.15 and Wed., Nov. 2 (view PSAT/NMSQT calendar).	Schools choose a date between Feb. 21 and April 14, 2017 (view PSAT 10 calendar).
Does the National Merit® Scholarship Program use scores to find eligible students?	Yes	No
Does the test connect students to other scholarships?	Yes	Yes

PSAT/NMSQT vs. PSAT 10		
Facts and Features	PSAT/NMSQT	PSAT 10
Who takes the test?	10th- and 11th-graders	10th-graders
Where do students take it?	At school	At school
When do students take it?	Wed., Oct. 19, 2016. Other options: Sat, Oct.15 and Wed., Nov. 2 (view PSAT/NMSQT calendar).	Schools choose a date between Feb. 21 and April 14, 2017 (view PSAT 10 calendar).
Does the National Merit® Scholarship Program use scores to find eligible students?	Yes	No
Does the test connect students to other scholarships?	Yes	Yes

As with any standardized test, the PSAT is structured and timed. The new PSAT/NMSQT and PSAT 10 include a reading, writing and language and math test. The test is now 2 hours and 45 minutes long, divided into the following sections:

- Math–70 minutes, 48 questions/tasks
- Reading–60 minutes, 47 questions/tasks
- Writing and Language–35 minutes, 44 questions/tasks

One of the key changes to the test is that it's evidence-based reading and writing that focus on the knowledge, skills and understands that research has identified as most important for college and career readiness and success (CollegeBoard). They placed a greater emphasis on the meaning of words in extended contexts and on how word choice shapes meaning, tone and impact. There is also no penalty for guessing.

The Score Reporting will be reported on a shared common score scale with the SAT: The scale ranges for the PSAT/NMSQT and PSAT 10 scores are 320-1520 for the total score, 160-760 for each of two section scores, and 8-38 for test scores. This scoring range can be challenging to understand. Visit https://collegereadiness.collegeboard.org/psat-nmsqt-psat-10/scores/structure to further understand the scores and stay up to date on any additional changes. Remember, only students in the eleventh grade are eligible to enter NMSC scholarship programs. But, you are also considered for other scholarship dollars through the College Board's new scholarship partners. There are millions of dollars available to qualified low-income and minority students.

Now here is a jewel, calculators are strongly encouraged. Your child may use a calculator they are comfortable with that falls in one of the three approved categories: four-function, scientific and graphing calculator. Because the test is timed, they will not have time to use the calculator on every question.

They may register to take the test with their guidance counselor or at any high school in their community. The test is usually given around the 2nd week in October on a Wednesday and Saturday.

- SAT (https://collegereadiness.collegeboard.org/sat)
- Nearly every college in America accepts the SAT or SAT Subject Tests as part of its admissions process.

The SAT test, also known as the SAT Reasoning Test, is used in the application process to colleges and universities in the United States. The test measures critical thinking skills and the ability to analyze and solve problems, and is often thought of as a measure of future college success. The SAT test is administered by the Educational Testing Service (ETS) at various locations across the country, and it is developed, published, and scored by the College Board. The test is given 7 times a year in the US.

The SAT is a 3 hours (plus 50 minutes for essay – optional) long test divided into the following sections:

- Reading–65 minutes, 52 Questions/tasks
- Math–80 minutes, 58 Questions/tasks
- Writing and Language–35 minutes, 44 Questions/tasks
- SAT Essay – 50 minutes, May be required as part of admissions for a university; otherwise, optional. It tests reading, analysis and writing skills; students produce a written analysis of a provided source text.

Each SAT section is scored from 200-800 each, 2 – 8 on each of the three dimensions for essay; yielding a total range of 400—1600 points.

Then you have SAT Subject Tests, which measures a student's knowledge and skills in particular subject areas, and their ability to apply that knowledge. This is the only national admissions test that gives you the opportunity to demonstrate mastery of content in five general subject areas: English, History, Mathematics, Science and Various Foreign Languages. Often times, this test is used by colleges to determine course selection and the appropriate level of placement. It also offers you an opportunity to show colleges what you know and what you can do. On the other hand, some colleges may specify the SAT Subject Tests that they require for admission or placement; others allow applicants to choose which tests to take.

All SAT Subject Tests are one-hour, multiple choice tests, but some of the tests have unique formats. Visit the College Board to learn more about these tests.

The redesigned SAT will report a total score, section (domain) scores, test scores, cross-test scores, and subscores. These Insight Scores reported are intended to provide additional information about student achievement and readiness that will convey a cohesive profile of student readiness. According to College Board, the list of scores, subject to change based upon ongoing research, is described below.

- Total Score: The redesigned SAT will report a total score that will be the sum of two section scores: (1) Evidence-Based Reading and Writing (200–800) and (2) Math (200–800). The SAT total score will be reported on a scale from 400 to 1600. The scores for the Essay will be reported separately and will not be included in the total score.

- Test Scores: The redesigned SAT will report three test scores, each on a scale from 10 to 40: (1) Reading Test score, (2) Writing and Language Test score, (3) Math Test score. The fourth test, the Essay, will be reported separately. Current plans call for the Essay component to report scores in three domains: Reading, Analysis, and Writing.

- Cross-test Scores: 10 – 40, Pending the results of research, the redesigned SAT will also report two cross-test scores: (1) Analysis in History/Social Studies and (2) Analysis in Science. Each of these scores will be reported on a scale from 10 to 40. These scores are based on selected questions in the SAT Reading, Writing and Language, and Math Tests and will reflect the application of reading, writing, language, and math skills in history/ social studies and science contexts.

- Subscores: 1-15, The redesigned SAT will report multiple subscores for Reading, Writing and Language, and Math. The Reading and Writing and Language Tests will each contribute questions to two subscores: (1) Command of Evidence and (2) Words in Context. The Writing and Language Test will also report two additional subscores: (1) Expression of Ideas and (2) Standard English Conventions.

You should always verify with the schools of interest their admission requirements, because things change and you want to be prepared and ready. In addition to reviewing CollegeBoard's website for recent updates.

- ACT (www.act.org)
- The ACT test assesses high school students' general educational development and their ability to complete college-level work. The multiple-choice tests cover four skill areas: English, Mathematics, Reading, and Science. The Writing Test is optional and measures skill in planning and writing a short essay.

The ACT lasts 2 hours and 55 minutes (excluding the Writing Test) and 3 hours and 35 minutes (including the Writing Test. The test is broken down into the following areas:

- English–45-minutes–Usage/Mechanics & Rhetorical skills–75 questions
- Mathematics–60-minutes–Arithmetic, Elementary algebra, Intermediate algebra, Coordinate geometry, Plane geometry, and Trigonometry–60 questions
- Reading–35-minutes–Social studies, Natural sciences, Prose fiction and Humanities–40 questions
- Science–35-minutes–Data representation, Research summary, and Conflicting viewpoint–40 questions
- Writing–40-minutes–You will respond to a question about their position on a particular issue

Each section is scored on a scale of 1-36, yielding a composite score between 1-36, as the average of the four sections.

In addition to this, like the SAT connects you to scholarships, ACT established a partnership with STEM Premier® in 2014 to enhance opportunities for all students, especially those who are underserved in the area of STEM (science, technology, engineering, and math). Through STEM Premier, students can qualify for scholarships funded through this partnership and build a profile to draw interest and recognition from colleges and business across the country.

WHICH TEST SHOULD YOU TAKE?

Almost all competitive schools accept both ACT and SAT scores. So, their decision should be based on the school's requirements primarily and then on the subjects they are stronger in. If all the schools you apply for accept both tests, you should then only take one tests. So, how do you choose, you may ask? The SAT is two-thirds critical reading and writing and one-third math. The ACT is one-half English and reading, and one-half math and science. So, if you are strong in English, you might want to take the SAT. If you are a math whiz and science geek, and not so good in English, you might do better on the ACT. The key is to take the test the plays to your child's strengths and give you the biggest advantage.

Here is a glance of the differences, although they are more similar now, between ACT and SAT according to Green Test Prep (www.greentestprep.com).

- **The New SAT doesn't have a science section. The "science" section of the ACT is easy to master, and has nothing to do with science. But if you hate it, then the New SAT is your savior.**

- **The essays are different.** Both tests come with optional essays. The ACT essay asks you to come up with your own argument and support it – the New SAT essay asks you to evaluate an argument that someone else has already written for you. Neither is easier or harder – it's just an issue of personal preference.
- **The New SAT has a few fill-in-the-blank math problems, and half of the math problems don't allow calculator use.** The ACT lets you use a calculator on all its math problems, and all the answers are multiple choice. The New SAT has a "with calculator" and "without calculator" section, and 13 of its problems force you to fill in your own answer. The "without calculator" problems aren't difficult because they don't require any difficult arithmetic, so it's not that much of an issue.
- **The New SAT is far less "time intensive."** This is the big issue that really separates the two exams. The New SAT gives you far more time per problem, so it's a much less intense testing experience. Alternatively, the ACT makes you go at a blisteringly fast pace. So if you need some more time to consider your answers, the New SAT is going to be your friend. If you can plow through questions and are super focused, then the ACT should be your exam of choice.

Once a test is selected, your child should plan to take the test early in their high school years. I say take it towards the end of their Freshman year to establish a baseline and get an idea where they are at. Then build a study plan from there that is focused on scoring high and improving the areas they are weak in. From there, make sure all tests have been completed by the end of their Junior year. Only take it during the fall of their Senior year, if they need to pull their score up for a school or scholarship. The goal should be to have the test scores they want by the end of their Junior year so they can focus on college applications the first semester of their senior year.

WHAT IS AN ACCEPTABLE SCORE?

The national average for the SAT was around 1500 on the old format and the ACT between 20 and 21; the new SAT average is yet to be determined. But, if your child's scores are close to these averages, they will likely be accepted into a college/university, as long as their grades are decent. It may not be their dream school or target school, but some schools will accept them. Remember the more selective schools will have stricter requirements, so, average test scores may not be good enough. Scoring above the average will improve their chances of getting into a more selective school, along with setting them up to receive merit-based scholarships. Keep in mind, the higher the score, the more opportunities they can garner.

Scores below the average scores are considered low for any major university. This can possibly be overcome with strong grades, strong essay, or an outstanding application. Even still, if accepted, the school may require children to take remedial courses as a freshman, participate in a bridge program, or require them to attend a community college and prove themselves.

After taking your desired test, you will be able to send your official score report to scholarships and universities. The rules for test scores are different for ACT and SAT. SAT has what's called Score Choice. This allows you to choose which scores by test date you want to send to colleges. If you decide not to use Score Choice, all of your scores will be sent to your recipients. You should still feel comfortable sending all scores, since most colleges consider a student's best score. ACT will only send the scores from the test date designated on the request. Choose wisely. But it's important to note, once you exceed the allotted number of recipients that come with taking the test, scores can be sent to additional recipients for a cost that varies.

Unless your child gets a perfect score on either test, there is always room for improvement. The key is to start the preparation process early, have them study hard and practice. Remember, high test scores can help garner additional scholarship money. Invest in a test prep class and learn the various test taking strategies, as it pays off royally. At the time of publishing, the newly released conversion chart was not out yet since the new format for SAT was recently released. But here is a preliminary table you can use as an initial guide to help define what should be your child's target areas. I am not providing the score conversion for scores less than what I call the "sweet spot" zone for testing. This area tends to yield some form of financial aid if coupled with academics, community service and leadership. For the latest updates, visit CollegeBoard and other sources for an official chart some time after May 2016.

ACT	New SAT (starting March 2016)	Old SAT (before March 2016)
36	1600	2380-2400
35	1540-1590	2290-2370
34	1490-1530	2220-2280
33	1440-1480	2140-2210
32	1400-1430	2080-2130
31	1360-1390	2020-2070
30	1330-1350	1980-2010
29	1290-1320	1920-1970
28	1250-1280	1860-1910
27	1210-1240	1800-1850
26	1170-1200	1740-1790
25	1130-1160	1680-1730
24	1090-1120	1620-1670

HOW DO I PREPARE FOR THE TESTS?

Your child can prepare for both tests first by mapping out and enrolling in the college ready course work during their High School years, covering the required subjects assessed on the tests. Then they must perform well in these courses by studying and working hard. Building a strong foundation for getting off to the right start really begins earlier than high school; around sixth grade – expanded reading, vocabulary exercises, etc helps.

Next, your child can take advantage of supplemental assistance through outside resources. Some of these resources cost hundreds of dollars, while others are free or charge a nominal fee. Proven resource options include:

- Practice Tests: there are plenty of online sites and books with free practice tests available to help your child prepare for the actual test. Some programs and resources include: My College Quick Start, The ACT Website, Test Prep Review.com, The Princeton Review, Kaplan, etc.
- Test Prep Classes: if your child don't do well with standardized tests, this option is highly suggested. The classes involve homework and practice tests. Classes are available via online lectures or in a physical classroom, administered by reputable organizations in your local area or you can try major companies such as Kaplan and Princeton Review. Physical classes are beneficial because they can assimilate your child better into a real test environment. As far as cost, there is a price tag usually in the hundreds or more, but it is well worth it when you think about the cost of college is at least $24k (avg) per year.
- Individual Tutoring: if your child need personalized attention to prepare for the ACT or SAT, this option is best. Having face-to-face interactions can help motivate your child to invest the time needed to properly prepare for the tests. Tutors can also tailor their preparation around their strengths and

weaknesses, while providing instant feedback and explanations.
- Here are some Test Taking "To Do's" that will foster an environment and discipline for learning.
- Study, Study, STUDY!–Create a study plan, buy some books and/or take a class.
- Register for the test by deadline.
- Visit the test center before their test to avoid getting lost, familiarize themselves with the testing environment, etc.
- Take a full-length, timed practice test about 3 days before the test. Remember, tests must be approached strategically and confidently in order to do well.
- Do NOT Study the day before the test
- The Day Before the Test, gather a "Test Day Kit" that contains (this can change, so always check the testing site):
- A calculator w/fresh batteries
  - A watch
  - A few No. 2 pencils with slightly dull points
  - Erasers
  - Photo ID (passport, driver's license, or student ID)
  - Do relaxation and visualization techniques
  - Get a good night's rest
- Follow The Morning of the Test Rules:
  - Eat a substantial breakfast
  - Don't drink a lot of coffee or liquids
  - Dress in layers so you can adjust to the temperature in the testing room

- Read something like a newspaper or magazine to warm up their brain
- Arrive early—allow time for traffic delays or accidents

6

MANAGING THEIR SOCIAL MEDIA BRAND

Technology is both a blessing and a curse depending on the choices you make and method of use…
choose wisely

– Tameka Williamson

In an age of convenience sparred by technological advancements, people tend to get more and more relaxed in their ability to think, analyze situations and problem solve. Compared to a couple decades ago, our culture has evolved from manual processing, Cassette tapes and VHS Tapes, physical workout classes, pagers and home cooked meals to microwave cooking, more To-Go/Take-Out Restaurants, Virtual Reality, Touch Screen Devices, Facetime/video chatting, Skype, etc. To top that off, we have social media and texting that allows us to locate and find people; communicate with them on a constant basis regardless of their geographical location. When you consider the cost and the convenience factor, this can be a great asset for people constantly on the go, looking to network, or connecting with relatives spread across the country. On the other hand, depending on how your child use these tools, they can live to regret their actions. Because young people often don't think about the consequences of their actions and/or the long-term affect, we are going to explore how the wrong actions can impede their future. We will break them down into the three main areas that have the greatest impact: Social Media, Texting and Phone Applications. How your child manages these three areas can affect their brand and their future.

SOCIAL MEDIA

From WhatsApp, Ask.fm, BBM, Snapchat, Instagram, Twitter to Facebook, these are just some of the most popular vehicles the younger generation use to communicate. Along with the youth, corporations use these platforms to screen their current and potential employees use of these same platforms. Facebook has a billion users and Twitter is around

500+ million users. More than half of children have used an online social network by the age of 10, according to a study. Facebook tops the list of sites that children sign up to underage, with 52 per cent of eight to 16-year-olds admitting they had ignored the official age limit, the Social Age report for online safety advisory website Knowthenet found.

Other popular sites include WhatsApp, used by 40 per cent of eight to 16-year-olds, BBM (24 per cent), SnapChat (11 per cent) and Ask.fm (8 per cent).

These platforms are used by many as means of networking, job hunting, reconnecting with friends and family, and keeping current on major events. The alternative side is where people use it as a means to brag, gossip, complain about their school, job, life, etc. or embarrass and/or bully individuals. Of course, these particular uses, along with the posting of inappropriate pictures are the activities that can get your child in trouble. Just like the phrase "What happens in Vegas, Stays in Vegas;" we can say "What goes on the web, stays on the web." Once it's posted to the World Wide Web, it cannot be erased. As a result, the improper usage can lead to expulsion, loss of a job, college admittance, a scholarship and worst yet, criminal charges. As you can see this is a serious matter plaguing our society, but not enough conversation is had about it. So, I hope the following information will increase their awareness. The same study mentioned above suggests that children are most likely to post an image or video of themselves online or set up a fake profile for the first time at the age of 11, try Twitter and message a stranger at 12 and try services like SnapChat and Ask.fm at the age of 13.

Furthermore, an Ohio State University article says, "College students who use Facebook spend less time studying and have lower grade point averages than students who have not signed up for the social networking website, according to a pilot study at one university." It was also discovered that students who use their laptops in their classes visits Facebook during class session according to Aryn Karpinski (Ohio State University Doctoral Student) and Adam Duberstein (Ohio Dominican University).

On the flip side, another survey stated that 70% of human resources workers polled admitted to not hiring a potential job candidate because of their internet behavior such as posting inappropriate photos and content on social networking sites. You may ask what is deemed inappropriate. Here are some examples.

- Pictures of them drinking and partying hard
- Video of them being drunk, carrying out sexual/provocative behavior (wet t-shirts, etc.)
- Use of Profanity on their page
- Comments that can be deemed threatening, discriminatory, racists, etc.
- Pictures of them with drugs or weapons
- Signs of cyber bullying
- Negative comments about their job, school, or person of authority

Remember there is no such thing as privacy when it comes to the internet and technology. It's all PUBLIC. Anything you post or text can be retrieved, even after it has been "deleted." They may think what they do on "their" own time is "their" business, unfortunately, that is not the case. Whatever they do on and off the clock of their job or school still represents them and their brand. S So, if their character and behavior is contradictory to their school/job image and culture (brand), a conflict is presented and the company/school will win every time. No company or school wants a person on their roster who will embarrass them and be a risk factor. Not only can this behavior preclude them from being hired, it can cause them to be fired, even after being hired. Please educate your child and challenge them to think twice before they disclose information on these social networking sites. This is not the place to air their "dirty laundry" and talk about the drama with friends, boyfriends, girlfriends, etc. You may say that there are no laws or rules regarding hiring and firing people because of their social media and that it may fall under the First Amendment, please understand companies and schools have the power to make whatever decision they choose as long as it does not violate any federal employment laws.

EXAMPLE 1

Heather B. Armstrong, AKA Dooce, matriarch of Dooce.com, is one of America's most popular bloggers. Armstrong was featured by Forbes magazine among 30 honorees on its list of "The Most Influential Women In Media" for 2009. Things weren't always so peachy.

In 2002, Armstrong was fired from her job as a web designer / graphic artist because she had written personal details and her various opinions of her experiences at an internet company on her personal blog. She did not fight the termination and she has never publicly revealed the place of employment in interviews. Armstrong is so well-known for this little incident that the site Urban Dictionary now defines dooce as "to be fired from their job because of the contents of their blog."

EXAMPLE 2

A man was fired from his job because he wrote very dirty things about one of his company's business connections.

EXAMPLE 3

A girl posted lovely pictures from her vacation on her website of her time at the beach which is the same time she called in sick to her job that morning.

EXAMPLE 5

Dan Leone, a Philadelphia Eagles stadium operations worker, was unhappy with the NFL team's decision to let Brian Dawkins, a safety, go to sign with the Denver Broncos. Leone vented to his pals on Facebook, declaring: "Dan is [expletive] devastated about Dawkins signing with Denver … Dam Eagles R Retarted!!" He later deleted the post, but the Eagles fired him over the phone a few days later.

EXAMPLE 6

Two young ladies graduated within the top 1% of their high school class and had GPA's above 4.0 had multiple scholarship opportunities. While interviewing for a prestigious university for college admission and a full academic scholarship, they were confident in their responses to the interviewing panel.

Unfortunately, the interview took a turn when the last question asked pertained to the girls Facebook page and the inappropriate pictures and comments on their pages. As a result, they were immediately disqualified and rejected from being admitted to this top tier university.

There are countless examples I can share, but hopefully, you already get the point and understand its importance and that EVERYTHING becomes public once it's on the internet. The process of monitoring social networking sites for content that may be of interest to employers and institutions is now part of the official process. Even so much that software has been developed and used to automate the process and dedicated personnel assigned to manage social media sites (Social Media Specialists, Analysts, Experts, etc.). Many top companies such as IBM, General Motors, Wal-Mart and Intel have implemented new policies around social networking. According to Proofpoint, of companies with at least 1,000 employees, 10% have disciplined their ranks for violating the rules; while eight percent of these organizations have fired at least one employee for egregious violations. Because most people do not read the fine print of the agreements and privacy policy on these sites, the best rule of thumb is to not publish anything via the internet you would not want anyone to know about or see. Social Networking has also opened the door to many other issues such as identity theft, the facilitation of pedophilia, harassment, infidelity, and others. Oh, let me not leave out the ability for police officials and lawyers to obtain information to aid them in securing convictions and win court cases because of the information individuals have shared via these sites. It is that serious and I want everyone to be informed of how something that seems to be so innocent and fun in the eyes of youth can have some detrimental repercussions. So, have a sense of decorum, respect and common sense when it comes to managing their thoughts, information, pictures, friends and networks. You as their parents have the power to control their environment and level of exposure and vulnerability. Monitor their accounts, stay in tune with social media trends and technological advancements. Familiarize yourself with strategies for keeping your college-bound student safe by viewing sites like Internet Safety 101 (www.internetsafety101.org). You especially want to be aware of apps that allow students to hide their activities.

In a 2012 study conducted by McAfee, it was found that more than 70 percent of teens have hidden online activity from their parents. Thirty-four percent of the respondents said they had done this using "hiding" apps, photos and videos. There are websites like WikiHow and Mashable that provide guides to the process and to the apps students use to hide online activity.

These notes are very clever because they go unnoticed most times, making it difficult for parents to identify them. For example, it may appear as a calculator on the screen, but it includes dangerous content. This app is KYMS (Keep Your Media Safe). By entering a password, the hidden content is unveiled. If the password is entered incorrectly three times, the app will secretly take a picture of the person trying to gain access and log the GPS location of the phone at the time the photo was taken. Then, there is a "panic" feature where the user can cover the screen with their hand if someone unexpectedly, like a parent, comes within viewing distance.

As a result, the app will close and return to its "calculator" costume. Another popular app is "Hide It Pro." It disguises itself on phones as an "Audio Manager." Even after you open the app, its true intention is still hidden. Until you pass the security protocol defined by your child, the user's content remains hidden.

Unfortunately, a large number of high school and even middle school students were identified as users of these apps. They used the apps to help them hide hundreds of shared nude photos according to lifezette.com. Hiding apps are also used to conceal other apps users don't want found on their phones. Examples of these apps include Kik and Whisper. Because youth have been known to share inappropriate photos and messages, their photos have likely reached the hands of sexual predators using the apps as well and exploiting students naivety. Parents, you must stay informed and on top of this matter.

Always err on the side of caution and consider their brand and what you want it to represent.

SEXTING

The use of cell phones has gone to a new level. What use to be a mode of communication for the elite, government and military officials is now a mainstream highly advanced technical device that allows individuals to not only use the phone, but communicate via email, texting, take pictures, watch TV, video record, project images, etc. etc. etc. As with anything that becomes a new concept, someone always finds a way to take it to the extreme and create a new phenomenon. How did the ability to send quick messages via the phone turn into a violent tool, I'm not sure. I can say one thing; texting is causing death physically and literally. Numbers are increasing when it comes to the number of deaths due to texting while driving and awareness has been heightened and legislation/laws created as a result. Awareness has also been raised for cyber bullying, resulting in policy creations. Unfortunately the other side of texting that is ruining the lives of many young people is not getting enough publicity. This issue has been termed "Sexting." Sexting, the latest trend among teenagers, is when a person takes a flirtatious, nude or semi-nude picture of their self and sends it to others through their cell phone or other means of texting device. Because this action often times entails the distribution of nude or partially nude pictures of a minor, it is considered a federal crime in most states. So, we are going to explore this dangerous craze so you and their parents are informed of the potential dangers that accompany sexting.

Everyone need to be informed, aware and concerned about the ramifications of sexting. Kids are sexting to strangers they meet online, boyfriends, girlfriends and potential companions. Often times they do this as a result of peer pressure from a "so called" companion or friend as a means of fitting in or keeping them as a boyfriend/girlfriend. Other times they do it just for fun. Either way, parents, you are usually not aware of their activity and the dangers it presents until the pictures are broadcasted across the school and internet and/or when the police come to arrest your child because of their involvement. That is why I am making this information public in the mainstream so everyone can be informed and take a more proactive role in preventing this epidemic from ruining our future generation futures.

This also ties to the hidden apps discussed in the previous section. The same level of caution applies to videos captured with their phone and shared on platforms like YouTube. Don't allow themselves to video activity that will land them in a criminal investigation. Nothing is "innocent" about capturing photos or videos involving racy, sexual or illicit acts or positioning's.

Teenagers are not only going to have their reputations ruined, but they can very well be arrested for distributing child pornography. The laws on the books have not caught up with technological advancements. So, this battle can be a dangerous and difficult one to fight. We don't want to resolve these acts to the common phrase "they are just kids being kids." That is not flying in the criminal system. Nor should you be naïve to believe "Not my child." Too much is at stake! Because, if they are charged and convicted, they run the risk of jail time and having to register as a "sex offender." Therefore, their future quickly goes down the drain because they don't finish school, can't go to college or military, and will have a very difficult time finding a job. Parents, you must also monitor your kid's cell phone usage very closely, often and implement controls. If you need advice and assistance on how to do that, parents you can reach out to your cell phone carrier for advice and look at software like Mobile Spy and Mobile Nanny.

We have talked about what sexting is and the risk involved, let us take it a step further and review the statistics around sexting to bring the dangers home with a sense of reality. The National Campaign to Prevent Teen and Unplanned Pregnancy and Cosmogirl.com published results of a "sex and tech" survey which explored the connection between teen sex and cyberspace (October 2008). The survey polled 1280 teens and young adults between the age of 13 and 26 about their cell phone, computer and digital device behavior and attitudes. Here are the statistics of what they found:

The percent of teenagers who have sent or posted nude or semi-nude pictures or video of themselves:

20% OF TEENAGERS OVERALL
- **22% of teen girls**
- **18% of teen boys**
- **11% of young teen girls ages 13-16**
- The percent of teenagers sending or posting sexually suggestive messages:

39% OF ALL TEENAGERS
- **37% of teen girls**
- **40% of teen boys**
- 15 Percent of teenagers who have sent or posted nude or seminude images of themselves say they have done so to someone they only knew online.

48 Percent of teenagers say they have received such messages

71 Percent of teen girls and 67% of teen guys who have sent or posted sexually suggestive content say they have sent or posted this content to a boyfriend or girlfriend.

21 Percent of teenage girls and 39% of teen boys say they have sent such content to someone they wanted to date or hook up with.

44 Percent of both teen girls and teen boys say it is common for sexually suggestive text messages to get shared with people other than the intended recipient.

36 Percent of teen girls and 39 % of teen boys say it is common for nude or semi-nude photos to get shared with people other than the intended recipient.

These statistics answers the question Why teens participated in this act:

51 Percent of teen girls say pressure from a guy is a reason girls send sexy messages or images; only 18 % of teen boys cited pressure from female counterparts as a reason.

66 Percent of teen girls and 60% of teen boys say they did so to be "fun or flirtatious"; their most common reason for sending sexy content.

52 Percent of teenage girls used sexting as a "sexy present" for their boyfriend.

44 Percent of both teen girls and teen boys say they sent sexually suggestive messages or images in response to such content they received.

40 Percent of teenage girls said they sent sexually suggestive messages or images as "a joke."

34 Percent of teen girls say they sent or posted sexually suggestive content to "feel sexy."

12 Percent of teen girls felt "pressured" to send sexually suggestive messages or images.

Because these statistics are from 2008, I am certain the numbers have grown and are increasingly disturbing in the days of 2016. Sexting have some serious consequences. Here are the categories of how sexting is termed in our state and federal government.

POSING A CHILD IN A STATE OF NUDITY OR SEXUAL CONDUCT

It is illegal for anyone, yes anyone – that includes teens (minors), to knowingly encourage, cause, coerce, solicit or entice a person under the age of 18 to pose or be shown in a state of nudity or semi-nudity for the sake of photographing them. So, when you see that statistics tell us 12% of the girls felt pressured to send sexually suggestive images and/or messages taken with their cell phone or digital camera, this is a violation of this stature.

DISSEMINATION OF PICTURES OF A CHILD IN A STATE OF NUDITY OR SEXUAL CONDUCT

It is illegal for anyone, including teens (minors), to knowingly send out or disseminate pictures of a person under the age of 18 who is nude, semi-nude and/or engaged in a sexual act. So, when 52% of teens have sent "sexting presents" to their companions and 44% sent images via a phone in response of one received, they have violated this stature. Going a step further, if a teen girl send an inappropriate image to her boyfriend and he in return distributes the image to other students and the cycle continues, they will all be in violation and considered someone who willingly disseminated pictures of a minor.

POSSESSION OF CHILD PORNOGRAPHY

It is illegal for anyone to knowingly possess photographs (in any format) which depict a person under the age of 18 posed with a lewd exhibition of genitals, buttocks, breasts or engaged in an actual or simulated sexual acts. Using the last example, everyone who received and possess the photo sent to their phone is culpable of this stature.

DISSEMINATION OF HARMFUL MATTER TO A MINOR

It is illegal for anyone to knowingly send to any person under the age of 18 matter considered to be "harmful. "Harmful matter" includes things that are obscene or pornographic in nature.

As you can see, this is very serious and many lives are being ruined due to a lack of knowledge and naivety to the fact they can be charged and possibly convicted for criminal behavior that is considered a felony. It is time to wake up and be aware of the risks involved with abusing technology and the intent it was created for. Although there is growing consensus among lawyers and legislators that the child pornography laws are too blunt for the world of adolescent cyber-culture, the behavior can still cause a student to be expelled from school, fired and unable to move forward with their career aspirations.

As technology continues to evolve and more and more cases of cyber bullying occur, laws are changing. Parents, please research the laws in your area and educate your child on them to help them not become a victim over what they perceive to be an "innocent" and "harmless" act. Their future depends on this knowledge.

7

CONCLUSION

If you want to be successful....
Don't seek success
Seek to become a person of value
Values is in significance
Significance in uniqueness
Uniqueness is in originality
Discover their gift
Refine their gifts
Serve their gift to the world
Education is for refinement.

– Dr. Myles Munroe

Their gift will make room for you
in the world.

The process of planning and preparing for College and positioning your child to be college and career ready is no small task. Nor is it easy. It takes a lot of coordinating, time management, organization, studying, hard work and discipline. The process can be tedious and nerve wrecking at times, but the end result surpasses the energy and effort put into it. Their reward will be far greater than you can imagine and it will be one of the best uses of their time. It can be the difference of $10K to $30K, if not more. Just imagine what your life and stress level would be if your child was in college fully funded. This is a wonderful feeling because I see the relief my families feel when this happens. To know your child is sitting in college and their $65,000 tuition bill per year is taken care of and they get a refund check each semester, there is no better feeling. I want this for you! Because, it is possible! I have testimonies and examples of families living this dream. You just have to be willing to put in the work and effort, alongside your college-bound child. So, Congratulations on investing in your child's future by not only purchasing this book but also by executing the strategies.

It is my hope that you find the information in this book valuable, helpful and practical for your child's journey to the next phase of their life. You will find worksheets to accompany each chapter in the Appendix section to enhance the learning process by allowing you the opportunity to put the tools into action. Don't be afraid to modify their answers as time progresses because things change and life happens. One of the keys to being a great leader is the ability to recognize and embrace change without getting frazzled. The key is to manage change and not let change manage you. Teach them to be the driver of their own success.

Follow the steps outlined, complete the exercises in the Appendix, checkout the suggested websites and books, and make wise decisions when it comes to paying for college, technology and social media. By doing this they will be well on their way to mapping out a successful future. Supplemental material can always be found in the "Resources" section on my website www.tamekawilliamson.com. You can also check out my partner website, National College Resource Foundation, for helpful information, scholarship, internship, etc. opportunities at www.thecollegeexpo.org. Subscribe to the newsletter, watch the videos, read the blogs and check out the free resources.

We'd love to hear from you, share your story. Or you can invite me to speak. Email us your comments and feedback on how *this book* aided your college planning process to booking@tamekawilliamson.com or via www.tamekawilliamson.com.

APPENDIX

GOAL SETTING

Part I. Personal Goals: Helps you focus on themselves, while developing goals that relate to their relationship with themselves. These goals will help you improve their self-image, enhance creativity, intellectual abilities, and shift their attitudes toward the positive.

Instructions: Answer the questions below. Be specific, open and honest with themselves. Then be specific in determining their plan of action and make sure it is measureable.

1. What attitude's or beliefs about themselves would you like to change or improve? How and when will you go about doing this?
2. What self-limiting thoughts or fears would you like to overcome? What steps will you take to overcome them?
3. What personality trait(s), such as being more dependable, would you like to cultivate, eliminate or better manage? How can you do this?
4. What is their biggest dream, hope, vision for themselves? What can you do to make this a reality?

5. What habits are you not happy with and/or you find are not productive in their life? What will you do to change them?

Part II. Based on their answers to the questions, list the most critical goals you would like to focus on . Then rank their level of priority as High, Medium or Low. Think of their goals in terms of Short-Term (1—90 days), Mid-Range (3—12 months) and Long-Term (1—5 years). Remember, goals must be SMARTR.

1.

2.

3.

4.

5.

1.

2.

3.

4.

5.

Educational Goals: Helps you focus on their education as it relates to training, schooling and certifications. These goals are meant to help you challenge themselves to improve their current educational level and strive for something higher.

Instructions: Answer the questions below. Be specific, open and honest with themselves. Then be specific in determining their plan of action and make sure it is measureable.

1. What GPA would you like to have on their report card in middle, high school, and/or college? How will you go about achieving this?
2. What clubs, organizations or sports would you like to join and excel in? What will you do to accomplish this?
3. What score would you like to get on their PSAT, ACT and SAT? What will you do to achieve this?
4. What do you want to achieve in their education (Dean's List, Who's Who, Valedictorian, etc.)? How will you go about bringing this into fruition?
5. What degrees would you like to attain (Associate, Bachelor's, Master's, and Doctorate)? How will you accomplish this?

Part II. Based on their answers to the questions, list the most critical goals you would like to focus on . Then rank their level of priority as High, Medium or Low. Think of their goals in terms of Short-Term (1—90 days), Mid-Range (3—12 months) and Long-Term (1—5 years). Remember, goals must be SMARTR.

1. _____

2. _____

3. _____

4. _____

5. _____

1.

2.

3.

4.

5.

Career Goals: Helps you focus on improving their career and professional achievements. These goals can be centered around starting their own business, achieving a certain position or even obtaining certain certifications.

Instructions: Answer the questions below. Be specific, open and honest with themselves. Then be specific in determining their plan of action and make sure it is measureable.

1. What leadership skills would you like to strengthen? How will you do it?
2. What specific things can you do, change, or eliminate to become better organized and more productive? How will you accomplish this?
3. What type of work would you like to be doing 5-10 years from now? What do you need to do now to bring this to reality?
4. What professional skills would you like to enhance (public-speaking, presentations, etc.)
5. What additional career goals would you like to achieve? How will you go about accomplishing this?

Part II. Based on their answers to the questions, list the most critical goals you would like to focus on . Then rank their level of priority as High, Medium or Low. Think of their goals in terms of Short-Term (1—90 days), Mid-Range (3—12 months) and Long-Term (1—5 years). Remember, goals must be SMARTR.

1.

2.

3.

4.

5.

1. _____

2. _____

3. _____

4. _____

5. _____

Part III. Select their Top 3 Goals from each section and list them below.

Personal

1.

_____

2.

_____

3.

_____

Educational

1.

_____

2.

_____

3.

_____

Career

1.

_____

2.

_____

3.

_____

Part IV. Complete a Plan of Action Sheet for each Goal.

Type of Goal: _____

Goal: _____

[ ] Short-Term   [ ] Mid-Range   [ ] Long-Range

Accountability Partner: _____

Why do you want to achieve this goal? List their reasons and prioritize them by ranking them from 1 to 5 with 1 being the highest and 5 the lowest.

[ ]
_____
_____

[ ]
_____
_____

[ ]
_____
_____

[ ]
_____
_____

Identify the risks that you anticipate on their way to achieving this goal. Prioritize their risks.

[ ]
_____
_____

[ ]
_____
_____

[ ]
_____
_____

[ ]
_____
_____

Identify the obstacles you anticipate on their way of achieving this goal. Prioritize their obstacles.

[ ]
_____
_____

[ ]
_____
_____

[ ]
_____
_____

[ ]
_____
_____

Identify the investments and sacrifices including time and money that you anticipate on their way to achieving this goal.

[ ]
_____
_____

[ ]
_____
_____

[ ]
_____
_____

Identify additional knowledge that you will require in order to accomplish this goal. Prioritize these activities.

[ ]
_____
_____

[ ]
_____
_____

[ ]
_____
_____

[ ]
_____
_____

Identify the people, groups or organizations whose help and cooperation you will need to achieve this goal. What role will they play. Prioritize their importance.

[ ]
_____
_____

[ ]
_____
_____

[ ]
_____
_____

[ ]
_____
_____

Develop their plan by listing everything you will have to do to achieve the goal. Prioritize their plan.

Priority	Activity	Target Date	Actual Date

Set a DEADLINE. On what date will you achieve this goal?

_____

Reward themselves for achieving this goal. What will their reward look like?

_____

_____

_____

Sign-off on their goals with their accountability partner to signify their level of commitment to achieving their goals.

_____	_____
Their Signature	Date
_____	_____
Accountability Partner	Date

Reference: This goal setting system is modeled after "What Are Their Goals?" by Gary Ryan Blair. Check out the book for more powerful questions and goal-setting categories.

LIFE PLANNING

Mission Statement

_____

_____

_____

_____

Vision Statement

_____

_____

_____

_____

Values Statement

_____

_____

_____

_____

Accountability Partners

1. _____
2. _____
3. _____
4. _____

Potential Obstacles

1. _____
2. _____
3. _____
4. _____
5. _____

Combat Tools/Contingency Plan

1. _____
2. _____
3. _____
4. _____
5. _____
6. _____

7. _____

8. _____

Note: Their goals should be linked and intertwined with this section. They all work hand in hand: Mission to Vision to Values to Goals to Accountability Partners to Potential Obstacles and Combat Tools/Contingency Plan.

RESEARCHING & SELECTING A CAREER

IDENTIFYING INTERESTS AND SKILLS

Here is a sample test you would see when taking an interests and skills profile test. As, there are many free test online, if want a book to refer to, you purchase Career Quizzes by John J. Liptak, Ed.D.

Interests

This assessment can help you explore career and job alternatives based on their interests. You will read each item, decide how much you would enjoy engaging in that activity, and select the appropriate response using the following scale:

4 = Very Interested   3 = Somewhat Interested

2 = A Little Interested   1 = Not Interested

This is not a test because there are no right or wrong answers. So, do not spend much time thinking about their responses.

How interested are you in...	Very Interested	Somewhat Interested	A Little Interested	Not Interested
Planting and trimming trees	4	3	2	1
Managing and protecting natural resources	4	3	2	1
Caring for sick animals	4	3	2	1
Working on a farm	4	3	2	1
Studying the composition of soil	4	3	2	1
Conducting experiments with plants	4	3	2	1
Section 1 Interest Total				

Skills

This assessment can help you think about and identify the skills you possess that you can transfer to the world of work and their education. You may have acquired these skills from working at various jobs or through leisure activities, volunteer experiences, hobbies, classes and trainings experiences. Use the following scale to describe the degree of skill you possess:

4 = Very Interested   3 = Somewhat Interested

2 = A Little Interested   1 = Not Interested

This is not a test because there are no right or wrong answers. So, do not spend much time thinking about their responses.

	Very Interested	Somewhat Interested	A Little Interested	Not Interested
In expressing your ideas creatively, how skilled are you at the following tasks?				
Singing	4	3	2	1
Dancing	4	3	2	1
Photography	4	3	2	1
Drawing	4	3	2	1
Writing	4	3	2	1
Debating	4	3	2	1
Performing	4	3	2	1
Designing	4	3	2	1
Painting	4	3	2	1
Section 1 Skill Total				

After completing the assessments, you would score each section to determine their rating (low, average, or high). Then their scores for interest and skills will be matched to occupations. This will help you narrow down their career possibilities. During this phase, you may find themselves having a high interest, but a low skill level and vice versa. Just keep in mind that just because their skill level is low in an area doesn't mean you should not pursue it—skill can be learned. But you should start out with those career clusters in which you have both a high interest and skill level.

For Example:

1. **Agriculture and Natural Resources:** An interest in working with plants, animals, forests, or mineral

resources for agriculture, horticulture, conservation, and other purposes.

Interests: _____ **Skill:** _____

2. **Architecture and Construction:** An interest in designing, assembling, and maintaining buildings and other structures.

Interests: _____ **Skill:** _____

Top 10 Occupations Based on the occupations you selected according to their interests and skill level, list the top 10 occupations you would like to explore in more detail.

_____   _____

_____   _____

_____   _____

_____   _____

_____   _____

Occupational Research Questionnaire: Take each occupation and gather more detail information in an effort to get a full picture of what is necessary for this field of study.

Occupation:
_____

Education Requirements:
_____

Job Forecast:
_____

Typical Job Responsibility:

_____

_____

_____

Typical Working Conditions:

_____

_____

_____

Salary Range:
_____

Work Schedule:
_____

Travel Requirements:

___

Related Occupations:

___

Training/Licenses/Certifications Required:

___

___

___

States with best job opportunities for this profession:

___

___

___

How has this occupation faired in the recession and/or poor economic times:

___

___

___

CHOOSING A COLLEGE/ UNIVERSITY/ VOCATIONAL SCHOOL

Target Schools　　　**State**

_____　　_____

_____　　_____

_____　　_____

_____　　_____

_____　　_____

_____　　_____

Top 5 Schools for Their Major

_____

_____

_____

_____

_____

Top 5 Schools in Their State

_____

_____

_____

_____

_____

School Questionnaire: Take each school and gather more detail information in an effort to narrow down and select the best school(s) for you to pursue.

College/University: _____

Location: _____

Major: _____ **Student Population:** _____

Ranking: _____

Admissions tests required: _____

Teacher to Student Ration: _____

Application Deadline: _____

Essay Required: _____ **Application Fee:** _____

Freshmen retention rate: _____

Avg. SAT/ ACT Scored: _____

Do graduate students teach freshmen? _____

_____

What is the percentage of class who graduates in 4 years?

_____

What does a typical freshman schedule look like? _____

_____

Is the school in a rural area? _____

Distance from airport: _____

What is the percentage of Greek Life on campus? _____

_____

Can Freshmen have cars? _____

Is there a bus system? _____

How Freshmen are housed—Coed Dorms, Single-Sex dorms, Honor Dorms, or Freshmen Dorms? _____

_____

What is supplied in the dorms (appliances, washer & dryer, desk, etc.)? _____

_____

_____

_____

How are roommates assigned? _____

_____

_____

_____

Is this a state supported school? _____

How much are out-of-state fees? _____

What percentage of need is met? _____

What is the make-up of financial aid packages (% of Free Money (scholarships, grants, etc) vs. Non-Free Money (Student and Parent Loans))? _____

_____

_____

_____

_____

Does the state have a reciprocity agreement, whereby those out-of-state fees may be waived? _____

_____

Tuition Costs: _____

Room & Board: _____

Miscellaneous Fees: _____

How many meals served per day? _____

What are the meal options? _____

_____

_____

_____

COLLEGE VISIT PROFILE

Date of Visit: _____

College/University: _____

Location: _____

College Admissions Rep: _____

Phone: _____ Email: _____

Financial Aid Officer: _____

Phone: _____ Email: _____

Guidance Counselor: _____

Phone: _____ Email: _____

College Dean: _____

Phone: _____ Email: _____

Observations

First Impression:

_____

_____

_____

_____

_____

The Campus:

_____

_____

The Dorms:

The Dining Halls:

Town/City and surrounding area of the campus:

The Classroom Settings:

Available Resources (Library, Labs, Career Center, etc.)

The Social Settings (Athletic Games, Greek Life, Community Events, etc.):

Parent's Thoughts:

Top 3 Likes
1.
2.
3.

Top 3 Dislikes
1.
2.
3.

COLLEGE COMPARISON SHEET

General Information	School 1	School 2	School 3
Location			
Rank information			
Web address			
Size			
Colleges and schools			
Other			
Applying	School 1	School 2	School 3
Admissions address			
Admissions telephone			
Contact person			
Application fee			
Date application due			
Send transcripts to			
Date application mailed			
Accepted?			
Accept or decline by date			
Other			
Requirements	School 1	School 2	School 3
SAT minimum score			
ACT minimum score			
Other standardized tests			
Grades			
Advanced placement (AP) scores?			
International Baccalaureate (IB) credit?			
Essay requirements			
Personal document requirements			
Resume requirements			
Community/volunteer work			
Other			

Finances	School 1	School 2	School 3
Yearly tuition (non-resident)			
Out of State Fees			
Books/supplies			
Room and board			
Transportation			
Medical			
Personal			
Estimated total			
Financial Aid Pell Grant			
Financial Aid - Student Loan			
Scholarship info			
Student employment info			
Financial aid office location			
Financial aid office telephone			
Other			
Non-Academic Student Activities	School 1	School 2	School 3
Club sports I'm interested in			
Greek system?			
Other			
Campus Visits	School 1	School 2	School 3
When			
Contact person			
Contact's phone number/e-mail			
Accommodations - Dormatory, Cafeteria, etc			
Campus Appearance			
College/Department Ammenities			
Surrounding Area	School 1	School 2	School 3
City, state			
Accessiblity to Mall, Stores, Shopping (miles)			
Accessibility to Airport			
Distance from Home (hours and miles)			
Average Plane Ticket			
Population			
Median income			
Average rental cost (2 bedroom)			
Top 5 county employers			
Average weather			
Notes:			

COLLEGE APPLICATION MANAGEMENT PROCESS

College: _____

Deadline: _____

Application

Date Submitted: _____

Date of Acceptance: _____

Transcripts

Date of Request: _____

Confirmation Date: _____

Standardized Tests

ACT

Date of Registration: _____

Test Taken (Date): _____

Scores: _____

SAT

Date of Registration: _____

Test Taken (Date): _____

Scores: _____

SAT Subject Tests

Date of Registration: _____

Test Taken (Date): _____

Scores: _____

Test Scores Requested To Be Sent To University

ACT: _____

SAT: _____

SAT Subject Test: _____

AP/IB: _____

Letters of Recommendation

Number Needed: _____

Requested From:

_____

_____

_____

_____

Requested Date: _____

Date Received: _____

Thank You Note Sent: _____

Essays

How Many? _____

Brainstorming Session: _____

Rough Draft: _____

Second Draft: _____

Final Draft: _____

Proofread by Someone: _____

Financial Aid

Deadline: _____

College/University Specific Forms

Information Gathered: _____

Copies Made: _____

Forms Submitted: _____

FAFSA

Information Gathered: _____

Copies Made: _____

Forms Submitted: _____

SAR Report _____

Verification

Call Admissions Rep and Verify Receipt of Application: ___
_____

Call Financial Aid Office and Verify Receipt of Application:
_____

Admissions Response Received: _____

Admission Acceptance Letter Returned: _____

Housing Deposit Sent: _____

Scholarship/ Financial Aid Acceptance Returned: _____

Declining Acceptance Letter Sent: _____

Declining Financial Aid Sent: _____

Thank-You Letter Sent for Scholarship: _____

Final Steps

Freshmen Orientation Scheduled: _____

Enroll in Classes: _____

Contacted Roommate: _____

Scheduled Campus Move Date & Travel Arrangements: ___

School's Suggested Reading List:

Date Reading List Completed:

ESSAY BRAINSTORMING PROCESS

Brainstorming is the beginning process to writing an essay. The process will help you generate ideas, think about their essay and give you a new context in which to view the subject matter. All thoughts are allowed when you are brainstorming. No idea is a bad idea, so write down everything that comes to mind concerning the topic. If you need further inspiration to get their creative juices flowing, ask themselves "why" to each point you write down.

Role Models

_____
_____
_____
_____
_____

Political situations that make you angry

_____
_____
_____
_____
_____

Political events or ethical issues that have inspired you to change their own life, behavior, or the world around you

_____
_____
_____
_____
_____

Characters from fiction that you'd like to meet

_____
_____
_____
_____
_____

Humiliating experiences you've had. How have they impacted you

_____
_____
_____
_____

Accomplishments you've achieved. Why are they important to you

_____
_____
_____
_____

Negative misconceptions people have about you

_____
_____
_____
_____

The best decision(s) you have made in their life

_____
_____
_____
_____

The worst decision(s) you have made in their life

How have you changed in the past three years

PREWRITING INTERVIEWS

Sometimes it's a challenge to identify characteristics about ourselves along with tooting our own horns. That is why you seek the advice and input of friends, relatives, teachers, etc. Here are some questions you can ask about two to three people to give you more info to include in their essay and use for their college interview.

What are three adjectives that describe me?

First Person:

_____
_____
_____

Second Person:

_____
_____
_____

Third Person:

_____
_____
_____

When were you most proud of me?

First Person:

_____
_____
_____

Second Person:

_____

_____

_____

Third Person:

_____

_____

_____

What do you think are my three greatest strengths?

First Person:

_____

_____

_____

Second Person:

_____

_____

_____

Third Person:

_____

_____

_____

What do you think are my three areas of weakness?

First Person:

_____

_____

_____

Second Person:

_____
_____
_____

Third Person:

_____
_____
_____

ADMISSIONS INTERVIEW QUESTIONS

Anticipating what you will be asked is a good way to prepare for an interview. Going through this process will also prevent the use of filler words such as: ums, ers, and I don't know. Practice answering these questions with family members and friends.

- ✓ Why do you want to go here?
- ✓ What do you want to major in?
- ✓ What are their interests?
- ✓ What books have had an impact on you?
- ✓ What are their strengths and weaknesses?
- ✓ What are their plans after college?
- ✓ How involved have you been in their community?

Sample Questions to ask the Admissions Rep conducting the interview.

- ✓ What is the mission of their school's President?
- ✓ How has enrollment changed the past 5 years?
- ✓ How and where do students fall short?
- ✓ What kind of students do you like to attract?
- ✓ What is the best way to succeed at their university?
- ✓ What is the best way to prepare for their university?
- ✓ What do you want students to know about their university?
- ✓ How many students apply each year? How many are accepted?
- ✓ What are the average GPA and average ACT Assessment or SAT I score(s) for those accepted?
- ✓ How many students in last year's freshman class returned for their sophomore year?

- ✓ What is the school's procedure for credit for Advanced Placement high school courses?
- ✓ As a freshman, will I be taught by professors or teaching assistants?
- ✓ How many students are there per teacher?
- ✓ When is it necessary to declare a major?
- ✓ Is it possible to have a double major or to declare a major and a minor?
- ✓ What are the requirements for the major in which I am interested?
- ✓ How does the advising system work?
- ✓ Does this college offer study abroad, cooperative programs, or academic honors programs?
- ✓ What is the likelihood, due to overcrowding, of getting closed out of the courses I need?
- ✓ What technology is available, and what are any associated fees?
- ✓ How well equipped are the libraries and laboratories?
- ✓ Are internships available?
- ✓ How effective is the job placement service of the school?
- ✓ What is the average class size in my area of interest?
- ✓ Have any professors in my area of interest recently won any honors or awards?
- ✓ What teaching methods are used in my area of interest (lecture, group discussion, fieldwork)?
- ✓ How many students graduate in four years in my area of interest?
- ✓ What are the special requirements for graduation in my area of interest?

- ✓ What is the student body like? Age? Sex? Race? Geographic origin?
- ✓ What percentage of students live in dormitories? Off-campus housing?
- ✓ What percentage of students go home for the weekend?
- ✓ What are some of the regulations that apply to living in a dormitory?
- ✓ What are the security precautions taken on campus and in the dorms?
- ✓ Is the surrounding community safe?
- ✓ Are there problems with drug and alcohol abuse on campus?
- ✓ Do faculty members and students mix on an informal basis?
- ✓ How important are the arts to student life?
- ✓ What facilities are available for cultural events?
- ✓ How important are sports to student life?
- ✓ What facilities are available for sporting events?
- ✓ What percentage of the student body belongs to a sorority/fraternity?
- ✓ What is the relationship between those who belong to the Greek system and those who don't?
- ✓ Are students involved in the decision-making process at the college? Do they sit on major committees?
- ✓ In what other activities can students get involved?
- ✓ What percentage of students receive financial aid based on need?
- ✓ What percentage of students receive scholarships based on academic ability?
- ✓ What percentage of a typical financial aid offer is in the form of a loan?

- ✓ If my family demonstrates financial need on the FAFSA (and PROFILE®, if applicable), what percentage of the established need is generally awarded?
- ✓ How much did the college increase the cost of room, board, tuition, and fees from last year?
- ✓ Do opportunities for financial aid, scholarships, or work-study increase each year?
- ✓ When is the admission application deadline?
- ✓ When is the financial aid application deadline?
- ✓ When will I be notified of the admission decision?
- ✓ If there is a deposit required, is it refundable?

SCHOLARSHIP APPLICATION TRACKING SHEET

Scholarship	Award Amount	Required Area(s) of Study	Created Application Checklist	Deadline	Application Date	Outcome

SCHOLARSHIP PROFILE SHEET

Scholarship Name: _____ Deadline: _____

Scholarship Source/Sponsor: _____

Web Address: _____

Contact Info: _____

_____

Requirements: _____

_____

_____

Scholarship Amount: _____

Is it Renewable: _____

Area(s) of Study Requirement: _____

Number of Recommendations Required: _____

Recommendations Requested by: _____

_____

_____

_____

_____

_____

Award Notification Date: _____

Submittal Checklist:

[ ] Completed Application

[ ] Completed & Proofed Essay

[ ] Recommendation Letters

[ ] Transcripts

[ ] Test Scores

[ ] Community Service Profile

[ ] _____

[ ] _____

[ ] _____

[ ] _____

General Notes: _____

_____

_____

_____

_____

_____

FINANCIAL BUDGET SHEET

Complete the grids below to get a complete picture of what you need to survive financially throughout college in comparison to how much money you have. This will help you determine how much money you need and how hard you need to work to secure scholarship and financial aid dollars.

	Contribution	Per Semester	Year	Gap
Job				
Parents/Family				
Loans				
Scholarships				
Financial Aid				
TOTAL				

This budget sheet is to help you forecast potential expenses for an entire school year.

	Expense	Per Semester	Year	Gap
Tuition				
Room & Board				
Books				
Meals				
Phone				
Internet				
Car				
Rent (off Campus)				
Utilities (off Campus)				
Travel Home				
Miscellaneous				
TOTAL				

COLLEGE PLANNING BUDGET

Monthly Income	
Item	**Amount**
Estimated monthly net income	
Financial aid award(s)	
Other income	
Total	

Student Name

Guardian

School/College

Monthly Expenses	
Item	**Amount**
Rent	
Utilities	
Cell phone	
Groceries	
Auto expenses	
Student loans	
Other loans	
Credit cards	
Insurance	
Laundry	
Hair cuts	
Medical expenses	
Entertainment	
Miscellaneous	
Total	

Semester Expenses	
Item	**Amount**
Tuition	
Lab fees	
Other fees	
Books	
Deposits	
Transportation	
Total	

Discretionary Income	
Item	**Amount**
Monthly Income	
Monthly expenses	
Semester expenses	
Difference	

TEST PREPARATION: TAKING THE PSAT, SAT AND ACT

COLLEGE EXAMINATION TIME LINE

8th Grade/ Freshman	Build Vocabulary—Vocabulary exercises, Word Games, and ACT/SAT Prep Books
	Enroll in AP (Advanced Placement) & IB (International Baccalaureate) Courses

Sophomore

Summer (before) Fall	Build Vocabulary—Vocabulary exercises, Word Games, and ACT/SAT Prep Books
Understand Test Taking Strategies
ACT/SAT Test Preparation Classes
PSAT in October for Practice
PLAN (Preliminary ACT)
	Build Vocabulary II—Word Origins, Synonyms, Antonyms
	Enroll in AP (Advanced Placement) & IB (International Baccalaureate) Courses
Spring	Understand Test Taking Strategies
ACT/SAT Test Preparation Classes
	Enroll in AP (Advanced Placement) & IB (International Baccalaureate) Courses

Junior

Summer (before)	Vocabulary Exercises
	ACT/SAT Test Preparation Classes
Fall	PSAT—Take actual exam to qualify for National Merit Scholarship
	Enroll in AP (Advanced Placement) & IB (International Baccalaureate) Courses
	Take SAT
	Take ACT
Spring	Take AP/IB Subject Area Tests
	Take SAT Subject Area Tests

Senior

Fall	Take SAT, if needed
	Take ACT, if needed
	Take SAT Subject Area Test, if needed
Spring	Register and Take AP Subject Area Tests
	Register and Take IB Subject Area Tests
	Enroll in AP (Advanced Placement) & IB (International Baccalaureate) Courses

5-YEAR COLLEGE PLAN TIMELINE

Status (S-Started, I-In Progress, C-Completed, NA)	Task Item	Timing
	8th Grade Year	
	Take an Interest/Career Assessment to discover possible career matches	Fall
	Start Researching and Investigating possible careers and schools	Fall
	Consult Middle and High School Counselors on Courses that ensure college readiness and smooth transition into high school - 9th grade	Fall
	Enroll in college prep and summer enrichment programs	Spring
	Start learning about Financial Aid Options and Terms and start preparing	Spring
	Develop a 4-Year Schedule of Classes per College Eligibility Requirements - Include AP/IB Courses	Spring
	Sit Down as a Family and Discuss College Plan and Financial Aid	Spring
	Research & Apply for Scholarships and develop a Scholarship Tracking Sheet	Summer After
	Visit a college campus	Summer After
	Create a Scholarship/Admission Portfolio (Brag Book)	Summer After
	Start Saving for College - if not already	Continuously

9th Grade Year	
Get Involved in Extracurricular Activities	Continuously
Take an Interest/Career Assessment to discover possible career matches	Summer Before
Develop a 4-Year Schedule of Classes per College Eligibility Requirements - Include AP/IB Courses. (Athletes) Check NCAA Elgibility Center	Summer Before
Build a Balanced Schedule that includes Studying, Extracurricular Activities and Other Interests	Fall
Look for Volunteer Opportunities	Fall
Start Developing a Resume and/or Portfolio of Accomplishments, Awards and Activities	Fall
Review College Plan and Financial Aid with Parents and School Counselor	Spring
Apply for Summer Job, Internship and/or Program related to Selected Career Field	Spring
Identify Test Prep Resources & enroll	Summer After
Create a ACT/SAT Study Plan	Summer After
Visit a college campus	Summer After
Work hard to Keep Grades Up	Continuously
Continue Scholarship Search and Update the Scholarship Tracking Sheet	Continuously
10th Grade Year	
Re-evaluate Course Selection to Ensure Alignment w/College Eligibility and Career Focus	Summer Before
Prepare for PSAT/PLAN	Summer Before
Take the PSAT/PLAN	Fall
(Athletes) Complete Online NCAA Registration	Early Fall
Continue College Savings	Continuously
Continue Working to Keep Grades Up	Continuously
Stay Active in Volunteer Activities	Continuously
Stay Active in Extracurricular Activities	Continuously
Continue Preparing for ACT/SAT/PSAT Tests - Execute Resources and Study Plan	Continuously
Continue Scholarship Search and Update the Scholarship Tracking Sheet	Continuously
Apply for Summer Job, Internship and/or Program related to Selected Career Field	Spring
Enroll in AP/IB Courses	Spring
Work, Volunteer, Read & Study for ACT/SAT	Summer After

11th Grade Year	
Continue College Savings	Continously
Attend College Informational Sessions	Continously
Continue Preparing for ACT/SAT Tests	Continously
Continue Scholarship Search and Update your Scholarship Tracking Sheet	Continously
Start Making College Visits	Summer Before
Re-evaluate Course Selection to Ensure Alignment w/College Eligibility and Career Focus	Summer Before
Sign-up to Take the SAT/ACT	Fall
Consider Taking College Prep Courses in the Summer	Spring
Start Asking Teachers for College Recommendations	Spring
Narrow Your College Selection List	Spring
Start Working on College Essays	Spring
Apply for Summer Job, Internship and/or Program related to Selected Career Field	Spring
(Athletes) Have High School Counselor send Official Transcript at end of Junior Year to NCAA Elgibility Center	Spring
Compile a List of Schools of Interest and Finalize College Visits	Summer After
Talk with Admission Representative to Determine Available Institutional Scholarships	Summer After
Discuss Final School Selection with Parents and Discuss Financial Plan	Summer After
(Athletes) Reach out to Sports Recruiters and Track Communications with Coaches/Schools	Summer After
Register with NCAA Initial Eligibility Clearinghouse and Compile a Sport Portfolio and Highlight Tape of Successes	Summer After
Stay Active in Volunteer Activities	Continously
Stay Active in Extracurricular Activities	Continously

12th Grade Year	
Create a Filing System/Workbook for all Financial Aid Documents and College Applications	Summer Before
Make Copies of Admission and Financial Aid Applications and Practice Filling Them Out	Summer Before
If Seeking Athletic Scholarships, Contact the Coaches From the School to Arrange a Meeting and Discuss Your Accomplishments	Summer Before
Create a College Admissions & Scholarship Weekly Action Plan that will keep you on Task	Summer Before
Request that Your ACT/SAT Scores Be Submitted to Your Final College List and NCAA Elgibility Center	Summer Before
Continue Working Hard and Maintain Good Grades	Continously
Continue Scholarship Application Process	Continously
Re-Take SAT or ACT (if necessary)	Fall
Start Filling Out College Applications - Be Aware of Deadlines	Fall
Gather Letter of Recommendations from Teachers, Coaches and/or Employers	Fall
(Athletes) Review NCAA Amateurism Status	Fall
Arrange Visits to Schools and Schedule Admission Interview, if Necessary	Fall
Confirm with School of Choice Receipt of Application Materials	Fall
Make Final Touches to Portfolio, Resume and/or Brag Book	Fall
Confirm that Your Transcript will be Sent to Your Colleges of Choice	Fall
Start Collecting Financial Aid Records for FAFSA (W-2s, 1099s, Bank Statements, etc.)	Fall
Register for a Federal Student Aid Personal ID Number (Pin) for you and your parents	January
Apply for FAFSA	January
Have Parents Complete and File Taxes ASAP	January
Review All Award Letters with Parents	Spring
Contact School Financial Aid Office of Any Outside Scholarships/Grants You have Accepted	Spring
Submit Your Mid-Year High School Transcript to Any College that Require this Information	Spring
Prepare for AP/IB Exams	Spring
Make an Enrollment Decision and Send Appropriate Deposits	Spring
Apply for Summer Job, Internship and/or Program related to Selected Career Field	Spring
Sign Up and Attend Summer Orientation Programs for Incoming Freshmen	Spring - Summer
Send Final Transcripts to Your Selected College & NCAA Elgibility Center	Summer After
Stay Active in Volunteer Activities	Continously
Stay Active in Extracurricular Activities	Continously
Stay On Top of All Due Dates	Continously

ENHANCE YOUR EXPERIENCE AND GET YOUR FREE COPY OF THE COLLEGE FOR FREE ACTION AND RESOURCE GUIDE AT

WWW.COLLEGEFORFREE.INFO

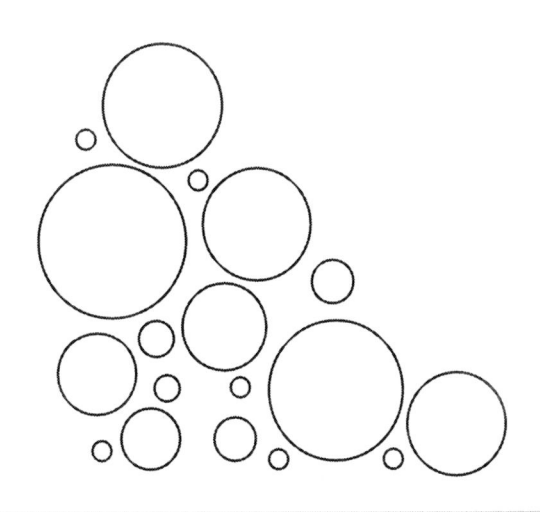

GLOSSARY

Academic advisor — This is a senior faculty member in their area of concentration who is assigned to advise you on course selections and requirements. Before you declare their major, you will be assigned a temporary faculty adviser.

Academic scholarships are based upon academic achievement as reflected in their college application.

Accelerated study — This program allows you to graduate in less time than is usually required. For instance, by taking summer terms and extra courses during the academic year, you could finish a bachelor's degree in three years instead of four.

Acceptance–the decision by an admissions officer or committee to offer the opportunity for enrollment as a student at a particular institution

ACT–a two-hour and 55 minute examination that measures student knowledge and achievement in four subject areas—English, mathematics, reading, and science reasoning to determine readiness for college-level instruction. (There is also an optional writing test that assesses students' skills in writing an essay. The ACT is scored on a scale of 1 to 36 for each of the four areas. A Composite Score is developed by computing an average of the four subject area scores.

ADMISSIONS DECISIONS

Admit — You're in! You are being offered admissions to the college to which you applied. Their high school will receive notification, too.

- Admit/deny — You have been admitted but denied any financial aid. It is up to you to figure out how you are going to pay for school.
- Deny — You are not in. The decision is made by the college or university admissions committee and is forwarded to you and their high school.
- Wait list — You are not in yet but have been placed on a waiting list in case and opening becomes available. Schools rank their wait list in order of priority, and unfortunately, the more competitive schools have years when they never draw from their wait lists. After a certain time, a rejection notice is sent.
- **Admission Deadline**–the date set by college admissions offices, after which applications will not be accepted

Admissions Process–a series of activities through which admissions officers recruit, identify, and cultivate relationships with prospective students, as well as review applications, make decisions regarding acceptance or denial, and notify applicants of acceptance or denial for admission to institutions or college-level programs

Admission Interview–a personal, face-to-face interaction between an admissions applicant and an institutional representative (admissions officer, alumnus, faculty, etc.) for the purpose of learning more about the applicant and assessing her/his suitability as a potential enrollee at the institution

Admissions Plans – Every college and university has a method for processing and admitting students based upon their enrollment objectives according to their admission deadlines. It is important to learn which admissions plan their college of choice uses to process their application and make admission determinations. See "Admissions Plans" in How College Admissions Works

Advanced Placement (AP)–High-level, quality courses in any of twenty subjects. The program is administered through the College Board to offer high school course descriptions equated to college courses and correlated to AP examinations in those subjects. High schools provide the courses as part of their curriculum to eligible students. Based on the composite score on an AP test, which ranges from 0 to 5, a college may award college credit or advanced placement to a participating student. A score of a 4 or 5 on the AP test is usually required by colleges for credit or advanced placement in college courses. A 3 is sometimes acceptable in foreign languages and some other subject areas. Some colleges limit the number of AP credits that they will recognize. Check schools' policies on AP credits.

Alternative assessment — This method personalizes the admissions process and offers students an opportunity to be viewed more individually and holistically. Less emphasis is placed on standardized test scores and more on the interview, portfolio, recommendations, and essay.

Alumni – a group of people who have graduated from a college or university

American College Testing — a not-for-profit organization providing the ACT examination program and other educational and workforce development services

Applicant–any student who has completed the application process at a particular institution

Art School (Arts College, Art Institute, Conservatory)– an institution specializing in the visual, performing, and/or creative arts

Associate degree — A degree granted by a college or university after the satisfactory completion of a two-year full-time program of study or its part-time equivalent. Types of degrees include the Associate of Arts (A.A.) or Associate of Science (A.S.), usually granted after the equivalent of the first two years of a four-year college curriculum, and the Associate in Applied Science (A.A.S.), awarded upon completion of a technical or vocational program of study.

Athletic scholarships are naturally based upon athletic ability and departmental needs of their prospective college. Division I, II and III college scholarships are very difficult to receive based upon fierce competition.

Award package — This is the way colleges and universities deliver their news about student eligibility for financial aid or grants. The most common packages include Pell Grants, Stafford Loans, and Work Study (see below).

Bachelor's Degree – is the undergraduate degree granted when a student has fulfilled all academic curriculum requirements as defined by their college or university and respective discipline.

Branch campus — A campus connected to, or part of, a large institution. Generally, a student spends the first two years at a branch campus and then transfers to the main campus to complete the baccalaureate degree. A branch campus provides a smaller and more persona environment that may help a student mature personally and academically before moving to a larger and more impersonal environment. A branch campus experience may be a good idea for a student who wants to remain close to home or for an adult learner who wishes to work and attend college classes on a part-time basis.

Campus Diversity–social inclusiveness that reflects variety in ethnic, nationality, socioeconomic, geographic, religion, and/or other group attributes

Campus Life–the demographics, academics, activities, social environment, and other features or aspects of the experience of studying and/or living in a college or university community

Campus Tour–a service provided by a college admissions office for prospective students during which they are allowed to visit various campus buildings, meet key institutional personnel, and get a first-hand look at campus life

Campus Visit–a component of the college search and admissions processes which involves the prospective student spending time on campus to get an overview of life at a particular institution (This visit may be initiated by the student or take place in response to an invitation from the institution.)

Candidates Reply Date Agreement (CRDA) — If admitted to a college, a student does not have to reply until May 1. This allows time to hear from all the colleges to which the student applied before having to make a commitment to any of them. This is especially important because financial aid packages vary from one school to another, and the CRDA allows time to compare packages before deciding.

Career College–"…a postsecondary institution that provides professional and technical, career-specific educational programs… Completion of a career college program can range from doctoral and master's degrees, to bachelor's degrees, to associate degrees, to short-term certificates and diplomas. Career colleges are owned and operated by private individuals, private investors and public corporations.…" [Source: Career College Association.]

Catalogue–a comprehensive publication that provides a detailed overview of an institution, including its mission, programs, costs, admission requirements, faculty and administration, etc.

College–"…an institution of higher learning that offers four-year undergraduate programs that lead to the bachelor's degree in the arts or sciences (B.A. or B.S.). The term "college" is also used in a general sense to refer to a postsecondary institution. A college may also be a part of the organizational structure of a university…"
[Source: http://education.state.gov/graduate/glossary.htm]

College Application–1) the act of seeking admission to a particular college or university; 2) the official forms and documents necessary for consideration by college admissions officers during the process of a prospective student's pursuit of acceptance at a particular college or university

The College Board–a not-for-profit membership association that provides a variety of services to college-bound students, to educators, and to parents (The organization is, perhaps, most noted for its administration of the SAT and PSAT examinations. College Board® is the trademark of the organization.)

College Box – is an exclusive email account on My College Options designed to deliver messages from colleges interested in you.

College Counseling–a student service conducted by a trained and/or certified professional to prepare students, as thoroughly as possible, for the transition from high school to postsecondary opportunities and, particularly, for enrollment in a college-level course of studies

College Entrance Exams–(There are two dashes here instead of the longer line like the others) standardized tests designed to assess students' knowledge and predict the pre-college student's ability to perform in college-level classes (These tests provide colleges and universities with standardized data for use in the college admission process.)

College Essay–a brief composition on a single subject that is required by many colleges as a part of the application process for admission

College Fair–an event at which colleges, universities, and other organizations related to higher education present themselves in an exposition atmosphere for the purpose of attracting and identifying potential applicants

College Major – is a concentrated field of study with specific curriculum objectives leading to a degree in the respective discipline. See Choosing a Major

College Planning–engagement in a series of processes and activities directed toward the objective of enrolling in college (This may involve self-evaluation, goal setting, the college search, preparing to pay for a college education, applying to college, making decisions about the acceptance of an enrollment offer, and other aspects of actually becoming a first-year, transfer, returning, or graduate college student.) The process of preparing academically, mentally, emotionally and financially for their future college education and career path.

College-preparatory subjects — Courses taken in high school that are viewed by colleges and universities as a strong preparation for college work. The specific courses are usually in the five major's area of English, history, world languages, mathematics, and science. The courses may be regular, honors-level, or AP offerings, and the latter two categories are often weighted when calculated in the GPA.

College Rep Visit–a visit by a college or university admissions representative to a high school or community site for the purpose of recruiting students for admission to the post-secondary institution

College Scholarship Service/Financial Aid (CSS) Profile–a service provided by The College Board to provide personalized student information to higher education institutions for use in their awarding scholarships and grants to students eligible to attend those institutions (The CSS Profile may be required in the application process for financial aid at some institutions.)

College Search–steps taken in the early phases of college planning in order to identify, locate, and investigate college-level programs that meet individual student interests, abilities, and needs

College Selection–the act of choosing and making the decision to enroll in and attend a particular college-level program

Common and Universal Applications — These college application forms can save students hours of work. The Common Application is presently accepted by about 190 independent colleges, while the Universal is used by about 1,000 schools. The colleges and universities that accept these standardized forms give them equal weight with their own application forms. Students complete the information on the standardized form and then submit it to any of the schools listed as accepting it. Some schools will return a supplementary form to be completed by the applicant, but most schools base their decisions on these documents alone. The Common Application is available on disk or as a hard copy and can be obtained from their guidance department. The Universal Application is available on the Web.

Control — A college or university can be under public or private control. Publicly controlled universities are dependent on state legislatures for their funding, and their policies are set by the agencies that govern them. Private colleges and universities are responsible to a board of directors or trustees. They usually have higher tuition and fees to protect the institutions' endowment.

Cooperative education — A college program that alternates between periods of full-time study and full-time employment in a related field. Students are paid for their work and gain practical experience in their major, which helps them apply for positions after graduation. It can take five years to obtain a baccalaureate degree through a co-op program.

Corporate Scholarships are awarded to help employees and their families, show community support and to encourage future job seekers toward a career in their area of business. Corporate scholarships are much less competitive than other types of merit scholarships because of geography, employment and the relatively low number of applicants. Start with their family's employers, check out the newspaper and see which companies in their area are awarding scholarships then contact these businesses and find out how to apply.

Cost of Attending College- the total cost of tuition, room and board, books, transportation, fees and personal expenses.

Course load — The number of course credit hours a student takes in each semester. Twelve credit hours is the minimum to be considered a full-time student. The average course load per semester is 16 credit hours.

Credit hours — The number of hours per week that courses meet is counted as equivalent credits for financial aid and used to determine you status as a full- or part-time student.

Cross-registration — The practice, through agreements between colleges, of permitting students enrolled at one college or university to enroll in courses at another institution without formally applying for admission to the second institution. This can be an advantage for students in a smaller college who might like to expand options or experience another learning environment.

Deferred Admission–a category of admission used in conjunction with early (action, decision, notification, or acceptance) plans to indicate that a student has not been admitted early, but will remain in the applicant pool for reconsideration during the review of applications in the regular admission deadline pool

Deferred Enrollment–a category of admission available at some institutions for fully accepted students who wish—for a justifiable reason—to take a semester or a year off before enrolling in college

Demonstrated Interest–a student's expression of his or her desire to attend a particular college, evidenced by campus visits, contact with admissions officers, and other forms of behavior that attract the attention of admissions personnel (Not all colleges use this as a factor in accepting students for admission. However, in 2004, the National Association for College Admission Counseling reported that more that 50% of their sample of 595 colleges

included demonstrated interests as a consideration in their admission decisions.)
[*Source: http://daily.stanford.edu/article/2004/2/5/demonstratedInterestIsUnfair*]

Demonstrated Need—the difference between the cost of attending a college and their expected family contribution

Denial–the decision by an admissions officer or committee to not offer a student admission to a particular institution

Departmental awards are for students entering their program or pursuing a degree in a certain field of study

Double major — Available at most schools, the double major allows a student to complete all the requirements to simultaneously earn a major in two fields.

Dual enrollment — This policy allows a student to earn college credit while still in high school. Many of these course credits can be transferred to a degree-granting institution, especially if the student maintains a minimum B average. A college, however, may disallow courses taken in the major field of concentration at another institution because its policy dictates that all courses in the major must be taken at the college. When considering dual enrollment, students should talk with admissions offices at the colleges they are considering enrolling in to make sure that they will accept credit transfers.

Early Action–an admission plan or practice which allows a prospective student to apply for admission according to an early deadline (before the regular admission deadline) and receive notice of acceptance, denial, or deferment with no obligation to the university to enroll, if accepted for admission

Early Admission–admission to college prior to completing a traditional four-year high school program

Early Decision–a plan of admission available at some colleges and universities through which a student may apply according to an early deadline and receive notification regarding acceptance, denial or deferment (The student agrees to make a commitment to enroll, if accepted under the Early Decision plan.)

Early Notification/Early Evaluation–an option offered to applicants by a relative handful of selective institutions to give the applicant some idea of their chances for admission (This is not an admission plan, nor is it a concrete offer of admission.)

Emphasis — An area of concentration within a major or minor; for example, an English major may have an emphasis in creative writing.

Enrollment–student matriculation, registration for classes and, when applicable, occupancy of college housing

Expected Family Contribution (EFC)–the amount that you and their family could be expected to pay for one year of college costs, based on the data gathered from the FAFSA and determined by a federal formula applied to that data (This figure usually differs from the actual amount you will be required to pay.)

FAFSA (Free Application for Federal Student Aid)–a federal form required as the application from all students who wish to apply for need-based financial aid (grants, loans and work-study)

Federal Pell Grant–a form of financial aid provided by the Federal government to students whose FAFSA indicates a high level of financial need

Federal Perkins Loans – are similar to the Stafford loans in that there is no interest accruing while you are in college. The interest is lower at 5.0% and the repayment grace period is longer than that of a Stafford subsidized loan. The "need-based" standards are more stringent and funds are awarded based upon the FAFSA Student Aid Report.

Federal Stafford Loan — Another federal program based on need that allows a student to borrow money for educational expenses directly from banks and other lending institutions (sometimes from the colleges themselves). These loans may be either subsidized or unsubsidized. Repayment begins six months after a student's course load drops to less than halftime. Currently the interest rate is 0 percent while in school and then is variable up to 8.25 percent. The loan must be repaid within ten years.

Federal Supplemental Education Opportunity Grant Program – is designed to provide additional need-based aid to Pell Grant recipients with greater financial need/lower Expected Family Contribution (EFC).

Federal Work-Study (FWS)–a program providing financial aid funds for students through their employment in part-time positions authorized by the institution and the government.

Financial Need – is determined by their family income, assets and the cost of attending their college selection. After determining financial need, their Student Aid Report will indicate the Expected Family Contribution (EFC).

Financial Aid–describes funds awarded to the student to help pay for his or her college education (Funds may come from the federal or state government, the college at which the student enrolls, or private sources.)

Financial Aid Award Package–an announcement package, presented to a student and his or her family once the financial aid process is completed, outlining the types of aid for which the student is eligible

First-Generation Student–a student whose parents have no college experience

First-Year Student–1) a college freshman; 2) a student who has not previously enrolled in a degree program at the institution and is not enrolled as a transfer student

Fraternity–a selective membership organization of male students at a college or university, associated for a common (and, in today's society, largely social) purpose or interest and, generally, identified by letters from the Greek alphabet

Gap — The difference between the amounts of a financial aids package and the cost of attending a college or university. The student and his/her family are expected to fill the gap.

Gap Year Programs–year-long programs designed for high school graduates who wish to defer enrollment in college while engaging in meaningful activities (Examples:

academic programs, structured travel, community service, etc.)

Graduate Schools – are usually within universities offering degree programs beyond the Bachelor's degree.

Grant–financial assistance awarded because of financial need (A grant may be provided by federal or state government, an institution, a foundation, or some other non-profit funding source and does not have to be repaid.)

Grant-In-Aid–funds provided to an individual or institution to cover the cost of a project or program or participation in a project or program

Greek life — This phrase refers to sororities and fraternities. These organizations often have great impact on the campus social life of a college or university.

Honors program — Honors programs offer an enriched, top-quality educational experience that often includes small class size, custom-designed courses, mentoring, enriched individualized learning, hands-on research, and publishing opportunities. A handpicked faculty guides students through the program. Honors programs are a great way to attend a large school that offers enhanced social and recreational opportunities while receiving an Ivy League-like education at a reduced cost.

Independent Counselor–a private college counselor who is hired by a student or family to assist the student in the college planning process by providing individual service and attention (It is important to note that, unlike college counselors and guidance counselors employed by the students' high schools, independent counselors do not have access to school records nor are they able to have day-to-day contact with the students and their classmates, teachers, coaches, advisors, etc. in the school setting.)

Independent study — This option allows students to complete some of their credit requirements by studying on their own. A student and his or her faculty adviser agree in advance on the topic and approach of the study program and meet periodically to discuss the student's progress. A final report is handed in for a grade at the end of the term.

Interdisciplinary — Faculty members from several disciplines contribute to the development of the course of study and may co-teach the course.

Internship — This is an experience-based opportunity, most often scheduled during breaks in the academic calendar, whereby a student receives credit for a supervised work experience related to his or her major.

Institutional Grant–a need-based grant provided by an institution and offered to students whose families are unable to pay the full cost of college (Institutional grants do not have to be repaid.)

Institutional Loan — any student loan administered by the college or university using the institution's funds as the source of funding (Perkins Loans may also be considered as institutional loans.)

Liberal Arts College–a degree-granting institution where the academic focus is on development of the intellect and instruction in the humanities and sciences, rather than on training for a particular vocational, technical, or professional pursuit

Loan–a financial transaction in which a sum of money is provided, with interest, to a borrower by an institution or individual (The funds borrowed must be repaid, along with the interest that accrues while the funds are kept or used by the borrower.)

Major — The concentration of a number of credit hours in a specific subject. Colleges and universities often specify the number of credits needed to receive a major, the sequence of courses, and the level of course necessary to complete the requirements.

Matriculation–the payment of deposits, tuition, fees, and other charges to enroll in a program of studies at an educational institution

Merit-based Grant – a form of gift aid (does not require repayment) based upon their grade point average, academic excellence and extra-curricular involvement with some attention to their financial need.

Minor — An area of concentration with fewer credits than a major. The minor can be related to the major area of concentration or not; for example, English major may have a minor in theater.

NACAC (National Association for College Admission Counseling)–a membership organization of over 10,000 professionals who assist students in searching, planning and applying for post-secondary college and career options

Need-Based Grant–financial aid offered, as a part of the financial aid package, when a student and his/her family are unable to pay the full cost of attending an institution

Need-Blind Admission–full consideration of an applicant and his/her application without regard to the individual's need for financial aid

Non-matriculated — A student who has either not been admitted yet but is taking classes or has been academically dismissed. Under this category, a student may neither receive financial aid nor participate in an athletic program at that school

Notification Date–May, 1…the date by which applicants who are accepted for admission to American colleges and universities are expected to notify the institutions of their intent to enroll and make enrollment deposits

Open admissions — A policy of admission that does not subject applicants to a review of their academic qualifications. Many public junior/community colleges admit students under this guideline, that is, any student with a high school diploma or its equivalent is admitted.

Pell Grant – the primary source of need-based Federal financial aid to which additional federal and state grants other forms of government aid may be added. Pell grants are typically awarded to students who have not yet earned a bachelor's degree. The maximum Pell grant award for 2008/2009 is $ 4731.00 but the amount varies based upon their financial need, the cost of their selected college, full or part-time student status and number of semesters you will attend in the upcoming year.

Perkins Loan–a low-interest Federal loan in which the institution is the lender and shares funding responsibility with the federal government(Both undergraduate and graduate students with financial need are eligible for the Perkins Loan and the loan must be repaid to the institution when the student graduates or is no longer enrolled as a student.)

Placement Tests–examinations used by institutions to determine the level of coursework for which a student is prepared and in which she/he is eligible to be enrolled (For example, such examinations may be used for placement in foreign language or mathematics courses or to determine if a student's level of competency warrants exemption from taking a course that is required for graduation.)

PLAN Test- is usually taken in their sophomore year to prepare for the ACT test. See full article on the PLAN test

PLUS Loan–the Federal Parent Loan for Undergraduate Students (PLUS) that allows parents (regardless of income) to borrow up to the total cost of education minus the amount of any other financial aid awarded by the institution or the government

Post-Graduate Degrees – are earned beyond the Bachelor's degree by completing Graduate school curriculum requirements. Common Examples include the MBA (Master degree in Business Administration, JD (Juris Doctor), MD (Medical Doctor), etc...

Private Institution–a college or university that is funded by private sources without any control by a government agency

(The cost of attending a private school is, generally, higher than the cost at a public institution.)

Private Organization Scholarships–number in the millions. Place of worships, labor unions, school districts, chambers of commerce and philanthropic organizations are all excellent sources for college scholarships. Sit down with their family and make a "scholarship search list", you will be amazed at the sources right in their own backyard.

Prospective Student–any student who is a potential applicant for admission… particularly those who have shown interest in attending the institution or in which the institution has shown interest

Preliminary Scholastic Assessment Test (PSAT test) – prepares students for the SAT and is used to qualify students for the National Merit Scholarship Semi-finals and other academic awards. See full article on the PSAT/NMSQT

Public Institution–a college or university that receives public funding—primarily from a local, state, or national government that oversees and regulates the school's operations.

Recommendations–statements or letters of endorsement written on a student's behalf during the college admission process.

Religion-Based Institution–colleges and universities established by and currently operating under the auspices, principles, or guidelines of a church, synagogue, or mosque; a denomination; or a particular religion

Reserve Officers' Training Corps (ROTC) — Each branch of the military sponsors an ROTC program. In exchange for a certain number of years on active duty, students can have their college education paid for up to a certain amount by the armed forces.

Residence Halls–dormitories, apartments, houses, and other living quarters provided for students by the college or university in which they are enrolled

Residency requirement — The term has more than one meaning. It can refer to the fact that a college may require a specific number of course to be taken on campus to receive a degree from the school, or the phrase can mean the time, by law, that is required for a person to reside in the state to be considered eligible for in-state tuition at one of its public colleges or universities.

Retention rate — The number and percentage of students returning for the sophomore year.

Rolling Admission–a practice used by some institutions to review applications as they arrive and the applicant's admission file is completed, rather than according to a set deadline

Scholastic Assessment Test (SAT) I: Reasoning Test — Also known as "board scores" because the test was developed by the College Board. This test concentrates on verbal and mathematical reasoning abilities and is given throughout the academic year at test centers. The maximum combined score for both sections is 1600.

SAT II Subject Tests — These subject-specific exams are given on the same test dates and in the same centers as the SAT I. More emphasis has been placed on these tests in recent years, not only because they are used for admission purposes, but also for placement and exemption decisions.

Seminar — A class that has a group discussion format rather than a lecture format.

Silent scores — The term is applied to PSAT scores because only the student and his or her guidance counselor see the scores. They are not reported to colleges. It is the "practice without penalty" feature of the test.

Standby — If a student registers for an SAT or ACT testing date and there are no seats available, the student may accept a standby position; that is, if a seat becomes available the day of the test, the student will take the test. The student must go to the testing center and wait to see if there is an open seat. A fee is attached to standby.

Student Aid Report (SAR) — Report of the government's review of a student's FAFSA. The SAR is sent to the student and released electronically to the schools that the student listed. The SAR does not supply a real money figure for aid but indicates whether the student is eligible.

Student-designed major — Students design their own majors under this policy. It offers students the opportunity to develop nontraditional options not available in the existing catalog of majors.

Transfer program — This program is usually found in a two-year college or in a four-year college that offers associate degrees. It allows a student to continue his or her studies in a four-year college by maintaining designated criteria set down at acceptance to the two-year program. It is not necessary to earn an associate degree to transfer.

Transfer student — A student who transfers from one college or university to another. Credits applied toward the transfer will be evaluated by the receiving school to determine the number it will accept. Each school sets different policies for transfers, so anyone considering this option should seek guidance.

Upper division — This term refers to the junior and senior years of study. Some colleges offer only upper-division study. The lower divisions must be completed at another institution before entering these programs to earn a bachelor's degree.

Virtual visit — This is the use of the Internet to investigate various colleges by looking at their home pages. A student can "tour" the college, ask questions vie e-mail, read school newspapers, and explore course offerings and major requirements on line. It is not a substitute for a live visit.

Waiver to view recommendations — The form many high schools ask their students to sign by which they agree not to review their teachers' recommendation letters before they are sent to the colleges or universities to which they are applying.

Yield — The percentage of accepted students who will enter a college or university in the freshman class; these students have received formal acceptance notices and must respond by May 1 with their intention to enroll. The more competitive the school, the higher the yield percentage.

RESOURCES

If you are looking for more resources, I encourage you to visit www.tamekawilliamson.com. Here you will find a host of articles, scholarship links, college planning links and a host of other tools.

If you need one-on-one college planning services, visit: www.tamekawilliamson.com or email me directly at booking@tamekawilliamson.com.

If you have questions or would like to share feedback and their testimonial, we'd love to hear from you.